DISCRIM WITHIN THE LIBRARY OF CONGRESS

The Fight Was Hard!

Class Action Lawsuit of 1975 on behalf of the
Black Employees of the Library of Congress (BELC)
Howard R.L. Cook, et al. v.
Daniel J. Boorstin/James H. Billington

"For God so loved the world, that he gave his only begotten
Son, that whosoever believeth in him should not perish, but
have everlasting life."
—John 3:16, King James Version (KJV)

Howard R.L. Cook

Former Employee

Published by
Howard R.L. Cook

ISBN: 978-0-578-80504-7

Library of Congress Control Number: 2020924354

Book Cover and Interior Design by
Lysa L. Phillips, LPS Marketing Designs, LLC

Scriptures taken from the King James Version". Copyright© 1982 by
Thomas Nelson, Inc. and cover image of the Library of Congress taken
from www.britannica.com. Used by permission. All rights reserved.

The author has provided facts from court records, relevant actions as
they occurred prior to the court actions and as the case moved forward
for approximately twenty (20) years, and his personal thoughts and
opinions based on his experience as a former employee of the Library
of Congress and the representative of the Class Action Lawsuit of 1975
on behalf of the Black Employees of the Library of Congress (BELC)
<u>Howard R.L. Cook, et al. v. Daniel J. Boorstin/James H. Billington</u>.

Printed in the United States of America.

For more information, contact howardcook86@gmail.com.

DEDICATION

This book is dedicated to the memory of Barbara Ringer (deceased), George Perry (deceased), Dr. Tommy Shaw (deceased), and Sylvia Gee (deceased).

These are the four (4) people who inspired me the most and gave me the most personal support. They gave of themselves to make the Library of Congress (LOC) a better place and truly make it the cultural center of the United States. They got into "good trouble." They got "in the way." If this country ever perfects itself to equal opportunity and equal justice as it claims; so, I dedicate this book to you.

ACKNOWLEDGMENTS

A special thank you to Marc L. Fleischaker, Esq., the lead attorney in the case, who was at that time, from the Law Firm of Arent Fox.

Marc became a friend and remains so until today. He could always put the human touch on the problem and not just the legal view. Many times, I needed the human touch. An example was when we were trying to establish the Cook/Shaw Foundation, which the Library of Congress opposed. The Arent Fox Law Firm is the same firm that supported Marian Anderson in 1939 when the Daughters of the American Revolution refused to let her sing at Constitution Hall in Washington, D.C. on Easter Sunday.

Many thanks also go to the other law firms, lawyers, and all the rank and file employees who helped me. I will talk about those who did not help later.

ABOUT THE AUTHOR

Howard R.L. Cook

Mr. Howard Cook is a former employee of the Library of Congress from 1960 to 1989. He worked as a researcher in education in the Education and Public Welfare Division of the Congressional Research Service.

Howard is a founder of the employee organization known as the Black Employees of the Library of Congress (BELC) in 1970. The purpose of this organization was to fight the Library of Congress for practicing racial discrimination against African American employees at the Library of Congress in employment.

In 1975, Mr. Cook filed a wide-ranging class action lawsuit against the Library of Congress based on charges of racial discrimination, which was denied by all the officials of the Library of Congress. Mr. Cook was not impressed and moved forward in the U.S. District Court for the District of Columbia. His efforts concluded with the court rendering a decision in favor of the class action in 1988 and 1992. Mr. Cook struggled for many years alone against the powerful Library of Congress management and the U.S. Department of Justice.

In Memory of...

Dr. Tommy Shaw

The late Dr. Tommy Shaw was employed by the Library of Congress from 1974 to 1999 as a personnel psychologist in the Human Resources department. His position placed him as a part of the Library's management team. No matter that Dr. Shaw was a part of management, he did not blindly back management in its discrimination against African Americans.

In 1980, Dr. Shaw filed a class action, which became a subclass to the case filed by Howard Cook in 1975. His part of the case was the first decided by the court in 1988. However, Dr. Shaw did not back off. He continued to provide expert support to the attorneys representing the Cook case until it was won in 1992 and beyond. Dr. Shaw was a different kind of manager and was never impressed by the claims of the Library's management that they did not discriminate on the basis of race. He persisted in his effort to obtain equal employment opportunities for African Americans and was one of those who dared to take a stand for what was right and just.

TABLE OF CONTENTS

DISCRIMINATION WITHIN THE LIBRARY OF CONGRESS

The Fight Was Hard!

Class Action Lawsuit of 1975 on behalf of the
Black Employees of the Library of Congress (BELC)
Howard R.L. Cook, et al. v.
Daniel J. Boorstin/James H. Billington

FOREWORD

In 1971, the world was changing, especially in the United States, because of the Civil Rights legislation that was being passed by Congress in 1964 and 1968, which outlawed discrimination based on race, color, religion, sex, or national origin–so we thought. It would take another Congressional Act, the Equal Employment Opportunity Act of 1972, to attempt to address discrimination against African Americans and other minorities in the workplace. It was a time when minorities and women were being hired in jobs that were not usually available to them in the federal government and private sector.

On November 1, 1971, I landed what I thought was a "dream come true" job. I was hired into the most prestigious division within the Library of Congress, the Congressional Research Service. This division provided research for members of Congress, their staff, and their constituents. So, I was proud to bring all my knowledge, skills, and abilities as a graduate of the University of Maryland, College Park, which was forced through the Civil Rights era to enroll African Americans. I was very productive and timely in providing factual information. Of course, this was done when technology was on the rise and at a time when you had to know what resources may contain the information that the members of Congress needed.

For a while, I was rising quickly through my GS (grade schedule) within the Congressional Research Service at the Library of Congress. I was training new hires, mostly Caucasians. They were getting more opportunities for training and education on the job as computers were becoming available as a research tool for information.

By 1975, I was beginning to see that I stayed at the grade level longer even though I was on a promotional ladder and could advance yearly to the next grade based on my yearly performance evaluation.

A problem was developing at the nation's warehouse for their employees to get information about what work performance was needed to advance from one grade to another grade.

When I was hired, some of my coworkers told me about an organization called the Black Employees of the Library of Congress (BELC) founded in 1970 by an employee named Howard R.L. Cook. Through his effort and other members of this organization, they saved the jobs of many African Americans, Asians, Spanish-speaking persons, and women. Mr. Cook was able to assist these employees by gaining information about the hiring, firing, and promotion policies from employees employed in key areas of the Human Resources department.

There were even sit-ins by minorities because of the Library of Congress' discrimination practices in hiring and firing. The Library of Congress became known to most minorities as "The Plantation."

In 1975, I had become a member of BELC. Things were about to change. Thanks to the members of BELC and Howard R.L. Cook.

In 1975, an administrative complaint was filed in the Library of Congress Equal Opportunity Office by Howard Cook and David Andrews alleging that the agency discriminated against all blacks, female, Spanish-speaking employees, and applicants for employment at the Library of Congress based on race, national origin, and sex. This administrative complaint formed the basis for the 1982 lawsuit, which changed the Library of Congress Human

Resources policies and helped pave the way for the first woman, Carla Hayden, an African American woman, as the current Librarian of Congress.

Carolyn Torsell
Former Employee of the
Library of Congress

INTRODUCTION

Howard R.L. Cook is a man of trust and honesty. He and I never worked together, but we were introduced to each other by a coworker and mutual friend, Robert aka "Bob" Felder. From that point on, Howard took me under his wings and taught me everything about how to go about getting people's attention. He taught me how to fill out an employment application, to file a complaint form of discrimination, and how to become a better person. Howard would always say, "There are many ways to skin a cat, and if people act like they don't understand you, then the next best thing is to put it down in writing." He said that everyone understands things in writing better.

Howard taught me how to file a complaint of discrimination in the Equal Employment Office. From 2004 to the present, I am leading a class action lawsuit against my agency with 900 to 1000 employees claiming the complaint of discrimination against them. I know for a fact that without Howard's help and his understanding of my situations, I would have probably left the agency or even gotten fired. I owe Howard a lot, because, without him, I don't believe that I would have been successful in filing my class action complaint and having almost 1000 employees feeling the same way, which made my argument just a little easier. Without Howard teaching me how to file a complaint, there is no telling where I would be. Howard's book is an example of his good work.

—Christine Mills

CHAPTER
1

THE LETTER OF COMPLAINT
November 25, 1975

This letter initiated the opening of the case of the <u>Howard R.L. Cook, et al. v. Daniel J. Boorstin/ James H. Billington</u>, 82-0400 C.A. at the Library of Congress (LOC) on November 25, 1975. The letter was written to Thomas C. Brackeen by David R. Andrews, a former employee, and Howard R.L. Cook, a current employee of the Library of Congress, at the time.

Thomas Brackeen was the head of the Equal Employment Opportunity Office (EEO) at the Library of Congress at that time. The EEO office kept the case from 1975 until 1982. They always claimed that the EEO office was investigating the case, but they never rendered a decision in favor of the plaintiff. The plaintiff filed a case in the U.S. District Court, District of Columbia in 1982. The case remained under the U.S. District Court for the next twenty (20) years.

Mr. Thomas C. Brackeen
Equal Opportunity Coordinator
The Library of Congress
Washington, D. C.   20540

Dear Mr. Brackeen:

This letter constitutes the Third Party Complaint of Mr. David
R. Andrews, 3070 30th Street, S. E., Apartment 103-G, Washington,
D. C. 20020, a former employee of the Library, Mr. Howard Cook, an
employee of the Library, and the Black Employees of the Library of
Congress and the undersigned employees of the Library of Congress
(hereafter Complainants). It is submitted directly to you pursuant to
Library of Congress Regulation (LCR) 2010-3.1, Sec. 12.

Complainants hereby allege that the Library of Congress, through
its officers, officials, and agents, has continuously discriminated and
continues to discriminate on the basis of color, race, national origin, and
sex against all black, female, and Spanish-speaking employees and
applicants for employment at the Library by:

> (1)   denying black, female, and Spanish-speaking persons
> equal opportunity for hiring by assigning them to the least
> desirable jobs and lines of progression wherein opportunities
> for training and advancement are limited while assigning
> white male employees of less or equal qualifications to more
> desirable jobs and lines of progression wherein training and
> greater opportunity for advancement is provided;

> (2)   utilizing job recruiting methods for supervisory,
> managerial, and technical positions which are designed
> to reach primarily white male persons and thereby insure
> that a minimal number of black, female, or Spanish-
> speaking persons will be considered for those positions,
> including but not limited to the practice of limiting the area
> of consideration for promotion to such positions to persons
> already employees of the Library;

> (3)   denying black, female, and Spanish-speaking persons
> training details and other experience building assignments
> which would enhance their promotability, while providing
> such opportunities to white male persons;

8

(4)   maintaining and utilizing testing, education, training,
experience, and other job requirements and selection
criteria which exclude black, female, and Spanish-speaking
persons from hiring, training, and promotion opportunities
and which requirements are not job related or necessary
to the safe and efficient operation and conduct of the Library's
business;

(5)   maintaining a promotion and training system based
upon the subjective evaluation of white male supervisors
which locks blacks, females, and Spanish-speaking persons
into discriminatory assignments and denies them equal
opportunity for promotion;

(6)   disciplining black, female, and Spanish-speaking persons
on a discriminatory basis by stringently applying rules and
regulations to them while ignoring or waiving such rules and
regulations with respect to white male persons; and

(7)   retaliating against black, female, and Spanish-speaking
persons for filing charges of race and color discrimination
against Library officials.

These acts, policies, practices, customs and usages of the Library of
Congress constitute continuous violations of the rights secured by the Equal
Employment Opportunity Act of 1972, 42 U.S.C. § 2000e-16; Executive Order
11,478 (1969); 5 U.S.C. § 7151 and 7154; and the Equal Employment Opportunity
Regulations of the Library of Congress of black, female, and Spanish-speaking
persons who have been, are, or will be employees or applicants for employment
at the Library of Congress.

Complainants therefore demand that the Equal Opportunity Coordinator
accept this Third-Party Complaint and expeditiously assign it to an Equal
Opportunity Officer for immediate investigation and assignment to an Equal
Opportunity Investigator. Upon completion of the investigation by an Equal
Opportunity Investigator, Complainants pray that the Deputy Librarian of
Congress make a final agency decision finding discrimination in regard to
each of the above-listed allegations and that the Deputy Librarian, thereupon,
take remedial action pursuant to LCR 2010-3.1, Sec. 13, including, but not
limited to:

(1)   ceasing the Library's use of the unlawful acts, policies,
practices, customs, and usages set forth herein and all
other such practices shown to be in violation of applicable law;

(2)   order modification or elimination of the Library's acts, policies, practices, customs, and usages set forth herein and all other practices shown to be in violation of applicable law so that they do not discriminate on the basis of color, race, sex, and national origin;

(3)   assign, hire, promote, or grant preferential consideration for hiring or promotion to all black, female, and Spanish-speaking employees and applicants for employment at the Library to those jobs they would now be occupying but for the discriminatory practices of the Library of Congress and adjust the wage rate, salaries, and benefits of black, female, and Spanish-speaking employees or applicants for employment at the Library to that level which they would be enjoying but for the discriminatory practices of the Library of Congress;

(4)   compensate and make whole by awards of backpay to all black, female and Spanish-speaking employees and applicants for employment for all earnings, wages, and other benefits they would have received but for the discriminatory practices of the Library of Congress; and

(5)   grant such other relief as may be just and proper.

Respectfully submitted,

David R. Andrews

Howard Cook

Black Employees of the Library of
Congress
Howard Cook, President

10

CHAPTER
2

COURT DECISIONS

The U.S. Library of Congress did not appeal either decision rendered by the U.S. District Court for the District of Columbia in the case. The case was <u>Howard R.L. Cook, et al. v. Daniel J. Boorstin/James H. Billington</u>, 82-0400 C.A. Two decisions were rendered by the Court.

1982: A lawsuit was filed in the U.S. District Court for the District of Columbia, by Howard Cook and a group of black employees against the Library alleging a pattern of discrimination against black employees and black applicants for employment in all personnel actions since 1975. The lawsuit titled, Cook v. Boorstin, was brought under Title VII of the 1964 Civil Rights Act, as amended.

1984: The court certified a group of black employees as a subclass. This subclass alleged that the Library discriminated by filing positions without competition under Section 4(a) of LC Regulation 2010-14.

1987: James H. Billington became Librarian of Congress and the case was renamed Cook v. Billington.

1988: The court enjoined the Library from using its noncompetitive "Section 4(a)" hiring or promotion authority except for limited periods of time. The court certified a class of black employees and allowed consideration of new claims of discrimination against blacks who qualified for professional and administrative positions dating from 1975: (1) competitive selections in professional and administrative positions; (2) noncompetitive promotions, such as career ladder promotions; and (3) other personnel actions such as training and other job-related opportunities.

1992*: The court granted the plaintiffs' motion for partial summary judgment based entirely on statistical data from 1979-88. Based on that statistical data, the court found the Library's three-stage selection process to be so "subjective" as to discriminate against black applicants for administrative and professional positions.*

1994*: Attorneys for the Library and the plaintiffs reached a tentative settlement agreement that provided for a total of $8.5 million in back pay, 40 promotions, and 10 reassignments. Included in the total monetary relief of $8.5 million was a total payment of $805,264.01 - the amount ordered by the court in 1989 - to the 4(a) subclass members.*

1995*: A four-day fairness hearing was held and nearly 200 individuals objected to the tentative settlement agreement, endorsed by both plaintiffs and Library lawyers after 21 months of negotiation. Members of the plaintiffs' Settlement Committee also testified to explain how they processed 2,134 claims and allocated $8.5 million in back pay, 40 promotions, and 10 reassignments.*

U.S. District Court Judge Norma H. Johnson issued final approval of the settlement agreement. She noted that "the sweeping personnel changes at the Library effected by the settlement of this matter are…the primary benefit produced by the Cook litigation." In her written decision, she noted that she would reserve jurisdiction over the action for a four-year period "for the purpose of implementing and assuring compliance with it and resolving disputes..."

1996*: The District Court issued an order allowing implementation of the settlement agreement. The settlement agreement became effective 12/1/1996 and was scheduled to expire 12/1/2000.*

The two U.S. District Court decisions favored the plaintiffs.

CHAPTER
3

SETTLEMENT AGREEMENT

The settlement agreement contained discrimination and segregation, putting a limit on the grade level of jobs to which employees could reach under the settlement. One example is the fact that no employee could obtain a senior or executive level position under the agreement and only one promotion could be obtained. The agreement was reached by the lawyers for the Library of Congress and the lawyers for the plaintiffs. There was little to no input by the plaintiffs. Dr. Tommy Shaw opted out of the agreement.

The author of this book does not know if Dr. Shaw was ever made whole. A starting amount of money should have been at least $50 million. Forty African American employees out of the 2,200 class action members each were given one promotion during the time of the class action lawsuit. The fact is that many African American employees were denied many promotions over the years in the lifetime of the lawsuit and before. No class action member was made whole. The class action representative had many factors to consider when accepting the settlement agreement, such as fighting other blacks who did not agree with the settlement and other blacks who did not participate in the lawsuit.

Because of LOC management, only about one third to one half of the settlement agreement was implemented. An example of this is the fact that no reassignments were accomplished, no transfers were accomplished, and no permanent legally validated job standards were accomplished under the settlement agreement. To the best of the author's knowledge, jobs at different levels are still being given out without competition.

UNITED STATES DISTRICT COURT
FOR THE DISTRICT OF COLUMBIA

HOWARD R. L. COOK, et al.,

    Plaintiffs,

  v.

JAMES H. BILLINGTON,

    Defendant.

Civil Action No. 82-0400
NHJ/PJA

JOINT NOTICE OF FILING

PLEASE TAKE NOTICE that the parties hereby jointly file the attached Settlement Agreement, with all Appendices, for preliminary and final approval. Counsel for the plaintiffs and for the defendant have signed the Agreement on behalf of those parties. The parties jointly recommend that the Court give the Settlement Agreement its preliminary approval on the grounds that the Agreement appears to be fair and equitable as written.

The Agreement provides substantial monetary relief to the plaintiffs. In addition, it contains measures directed towards the Library of Congress' competitive and noncompetitive selections and personnel actions. It provides for record keeping and review by the Office of Personnel Management at the conclusion of one year after Final Court Approval. Moreover, a number of key provisions in the Agreement will take effect upon Preliminary Court Approval, for example the Competitive Selection Procedures contained in paragraph 3 of the Agreement. After Preliminary Court Approval, all potential class members and employees of the Library will be notified as provided in paragraphs 18, 19, 22, and 23.

16

The parties further request that the Court schedule a Fairness Hearing during which any objections or concerns regarding this Agreement may be aired. By the terms of this Agreement, the Fairness Hearing may be scheduled no less than 225 days from the date of Preliminary Court Approval and no less than 60 days after submission of the report referenced in paragraphs 20, 22 and 23. Accordingly, if the Court grants preliminary Court approval on or after August 2, 1994, the Fairness Hearing should be scheduled on or after March 15, 1995. A Notice of Fairness Hearing for the Court's signature is attached to the Settlement Agreement as Appendix F.

Respectfully Submitted,

MARC L. FLEISCHAKER
D.C. Bar #4333
DAVID L. KELLEHER
D.C. Bar #388661
MINDY L. KLASKY
D.C. Bar #426589
Arent Fox Kintner
    Plotkin & Kahn
1050 Connecticut Ave., N.W.
Washington, D.C. 20036
(202) 857-6000

ERIC H. HOLDER, JR.
D.C. Bar # 303115
United States Attorney

JOHN D. 'BATES
D.C. Bar #934927
Assistant United States Attorney

JOHN OLIVER BIRCH
D.C. Bar #234419
Assistant United States Attorney

MADELYN E. JOHNSON
D.C. Bar #292318
Assistant United States Attorney
555 4th Street, N.W.
10th Floor
Washington, D.C. 20001
(202) 514-7135

JOSEPH M. SELLERS
D.C. Bar #318410

- 2 -

17

AVIS E. BUCHANAN
D.C. Bar #365208
Washington Lawyers
  Committee for Civil
  Rights and Urban Affairs
1300 19th Street, N.W.
Suite 500
Washington, D.C. 20036
(202) 835-0031

Counsel for Plaintiffs

LANA KAY JONES
D.C. Bar #929083
Associate General Counsel
Library of Congress
Washington, D.C. 20540
(202) 707-6316

Counsel for Defendant

CERTIFICATE OF SERVICE

I HEREBY CERTIFY that on this 1ˢᵗ day of August ,
1994, the foregoing was served on counsel for Dr. Tommy Shaw by
causing a copy to be mailed, postage prepaid, and addressed:

John W. Davis
1730 K Street, N.W.
Suite 304
Washington, D.C. 20006

MADELYN E. JOHNSON, DC BAR #292318
Assistant United States Attorney
Judiciary Center Bldg., Rm. 4213
555 4th Street, N.W.
Washington, D.C.   20001
(202) 514-7135

- 4 -

HOWARD R.L. COOK, et al.,

Plaintiffs,

v.   C.A. No. 82-0400 (NHJ/PJA)

JAMES H. BILLINGTON,

Defendant.

SETTLEMENT AGREEMENT

This Settlement Agreement is entered into this ___ day of
_____, 1994, between plaintiffs Howard R. L. Cook, et al.
(hereinafter collectively referred to as "Plaintiffs"), by and
through their undersigned counsel, and defendant James H.
Billington, the Librarian of Congress (hereinafter referred to as
"Defendant"), by and through his undersigned counsel, for the
purpose of terminating all aspects of this class action. In the
interest of avoiding the expense, delay, and inconvenience of
further litigation of the issues raised in this action, and in
consideration of the mutual promises, covenants, and obligations
in this Agreement, and for good and valuable consideration, the
receipt and adequacy of which are acknowledged, plaintiffs and
defendant hereby stipulate and agree as follows, subject to the
approval of the Court.

20

I. DEFINITIONS AND GENERAL PROVISIONS

1. The following terms are defined as follows:

A. "Agreement" and "Settlement Agreement" -- These terms refer to this Settlement Agreement and all attachments thereto.

B. "Duration of this Agreement" -- This term refers to the period described in Section X.

C. "Effective Date of this Agreement" -- This term refers to the date of Final Court Approval of this Agreement.

D. "Final Court Approval" -- This term refers to that date, following the conduct of a Fairness Hearing and approval of this Agreement by the Court, on which any and all appeals from any objections to the Agreement have been dismissed, a final appellate decision upholding approval has been rendered, or the time for taking an appeal has expired without an appeal having been taken. If there are no objections to the Agreement, this term refers to that date, following the conduct of the Fairness Hearing, on which the Court grants final approval of the Agreement.

E. "Professional" and "Administrative" -- These terms refer to: (1) the professional and administrative positions as defined by the Office of Personnel Management and relate to the job series created by the Classification Act, 5 U.S.C. § 5100; and (2) all supervisory positions in any technical series as set forth in Appendix A which is incorporated herein.

- 2 -

21

F.   "Preliminary Court Approval" -- This term refers
to that date, following submission of this Agreement to the Court
by the parties but prior to the conduct of a Fairness Hearing, on
which the Court grants initial approval of the Agreement.

G.   "Plaintiffs", "Plaintiff Class" or "Class
Members" -- These terms refer to (i) the class of plaintiffs
certified by the District Court on December 13, 1988 as follows:

> All past, present and future black employees
> at the Library of Congress who possess the
> minimum objective qualifications necessary to
> be eligible under valid, nondiscriminatory
> standards for selection or promotion to any
> professional or administrative position at
> the Library of Congress, and who have been,
> are being, or may in the future be, denied
> equal employment or promotional opportunities
> as a result of defendant's discriminatory
> practices complained of herein.

see December 13, 1988 Opinion at 3, and (ii) include all members
of the 4(a) Subclass certified by the Court on June 8, 1984 as:

> All past, present and future black employees
> at the Library of Congress ...
>
>   * * *
>
> who were not promoted to positions by reason
> of the Library of Congress Regulations,
> section 4(a).

see June 8, 1984 Opinion at 3-4; provided that individuals who
fall within either, or both, of the descriptions quoted above
were employed by the Library of Congress on or after November 25,
1975 and on or before the date of Preliminary Court Approval of
this Agreement. The class as certified and defined in this
Agreement refers only to actual employees of the Library of

- 3 -

22

Congress during the time period described herein and does not refer to outside applicants for employment.

H. "Plaintiffs' Counsel" -- This term refers to Plaintiffs' class counsel: Arent Fox Kintner Plotkin & Kahn and the Washington Lawyers' Committee for Civil Rights and Urban Affairs. "Counsel For The Parties" refers to counsel for the Plaintiff Class and counsel for the Defendant.

I. "Defendant" and "Library" -- These terms refer to the Library of Congress and the Librarian of Congress in his official capacity as Librarian.

J. "Uniform Guidelines" -- This term refers to the Uniform Guidelines on Employee Selection Procedures, 29 C.F.R. Part 1607 (1978). Except as otherwise stated in this Agreement, nothing contained in this Agreement shall obligate the Library to apply the Uniform Guidelines to personnel selections or to personnel actions. The parties agree that under this Agreement the Four-Fifths Rule of Section 1607.4D shall be applied only as set forth in Paragraph 3(C)(ii), below. The parties further agree that, as used in this Agreement, the term Uniform Guidelines does not include the following sections: 29 C.F.R. §§ 1607.6, 1607.10, 1607.17, and 1607.18. In all other respects, the Uniform Guidelines shall apply as stated herein. To the extent the terms of this Agreement conflict with 29 C.F.R. Part 1607, the Agreement shall govern. With regard to questions of interpretation of the Uniform Guidelines, the parties agree to utilize the Questions and Answers on Uniform Guidelines on

- 4 -

23

Employee Selection Procedures, 44 Fed. Reg. 11996 (March 2, 1979), or other applicable authority.

2.   Except as otherwise stated in this Agreement, nothing contained in this Agreement shall obligate, require, authorize, or permit the Library to grant to any person a preference in promotion, selection, or any other employment practice on the basis of race, color, or national origin. Similarly, except as otherwise stated in this Agreement, nothing contained in this Agreement shall obligate the Library to create new positions, to fill any particular position, or to promote, select, or non-competitively assign any particular person.

II. COMPETITIVE SELECTIONS

3.   A.   Immediately upon Preliminary Court Approval and continuing for the Duration of this Agreement, the Defendant shall create, advertise, post, and fill all competitive selections for Professional and Administrative positions, regardless of grade level, pursuant to selection procedures that are in accordance with (i) the Uniform Guidelines; (ii) the attached Appendix B, incorporated herein, as amended from time to time in accordance with the terms of this Agreement; and (iii) the Library's Human Resources Directives and any other relevant Library regulations.

B.   When validation is conducted by means other than content validation, it shall be conducted pursuant to procedures

- 5 -

24

reviewed by Plaintiffs' Counsel and in accordance with the Uniform Guidelines.

C. Beginning not later than the Effective Date of this Agreement, and continuing through the final quarter of this Agreement, on a quarterly basis the Library shall review the results of the selection procedures for the preceding quarter together with the four immediately preceding quarters for which data has been maintained, using standard statistical measures, to determine if there has been any disparate impact on African-Americans. Upon their creation, these statistical analyses shall be provided to Plaintiffs' Counsel. The final report pursuant to this Paragraph shall cover the final quarter preceding the expiration of this Agreement.

(i) Except in those instances when the number of selections made in any five-quarter period is too small to permit a meaningful statistical analysis if the statistics for the five quarters under review pursuant to this paragraph show a disparate impact, namely, a showing of 1.96 standard deviations or greater, the Library will analyze the reasons for it and take appropriate corrective action in conformance with the Uniform Guidelines.

(ii) If the number of competitive selections made in any five-quarter period is too small to permit a meaningful statistical analysis, as described in subsection (C)(i), above, the Library shall apply the "Four-Fifths Rule" as set forth in the Uniform Guidelines at section 1607.4D. If application of the Four-Fifths Rule shows, in any two consecutive quarters, that the

- 6 -

selection rate for African-American employees was less than would be expected following application of the Four Fifths Rule, then the Library shall undertake a Multiple Pools Statistical Analysis to determine the extent, if any, of possible disparate impact. If the Multiple Pools Statistical Analysis reveals a statistically significant disparate impact, then the Library shall analyze the reasons for it and take appropriate corrective action in conformance with the Uniform Guidelines.

(iii) If the Library's implementation of its selection procedures is in compliance with this Agreement, and the selection procedures are not changed except as set forth in this Agreement, the selection procedures shall not be subject to challenge by Plaintiffs until at least one year from the Effective Date of this Agreement.

D. All competitive selections for Professional and Administrative positions shall be made in accordance with the procedures set forth in paragraph 3A above, unless:

(i) Plaintiffs' Counsel agrees to specific exceptions; or

(ii) Pursuant to a developmental, training, or affirmative action program that has been reviewed by Plaintiffs' Counsel and has been duly promulgated and/or negotiated with the relevant labor organization(s), different procedures are necessary to achieve the goal of the specific program and that goal is consistent with the goal of job-related non-discriminatory selections.

- 7 -

E. For the Duration of this Agreement, the Library
agrees to provide to Plaintiffs' Counsel any amendments to now-
existing Human Resources Directives, any newly issued additions
to the Library's Human Resources Directives, and any other
relevant Library regulations prior to their effective date. All
such directives, amendments, etc. shall be subject to Review by
Plaintiffs' Counsel pursuant to Section XV.

III. NON-COMPETITIVE PERSONNEL ACTIONS

4. Upon the Effective Date of this Agreement, and as
necessary for the Duration of this Agreement, the Library shall
issue Human Resources Directives, or other Library regulations,
to ensure that non-competitive personnel actions (including, but
not limited to, career ladder promotions, details, transfers,
temporary appointments, temporary promotions, reclassifications,
and reassignments) are based on legitimate, non-discriminatory,
job-related criteria. All such directives and regulations, and
their application in particular personnel actions, shall be
subject to Review by Plaintiffs' Counsel prior to issuance.

IV. PROFESSIONAL DEVELOPMENT AND TRAINING

5. The Library shall provide training to all supervisors
that shall include: Equal Employment Opportunity training;
training on the changes in the Library's competitive selection
process and non-competitive personnel actions; training about

- 8 -

27

techniques for managing a diverse workforce; and training about unlawful stereotyping.

6.   All participants in the above-described competitive selection procedures, including human resource specialists, panel members, and selecting officials, also shall be trained in the selection procedures prior to their participation. As a part of this training, all participants shall also receive Equal Employment Opportunity training emphasizing the need for job-relatedness promoting diversity.

V.   ACCESS TO MANAGEMENT

7.   For the Duration of this Agreement, the Plaintiffs shall have the option of meeting with Library management not less than twice annually at a mutually agreeable time. The attendees at the meetings shall include (a) three to six class representatives chosen by whatever means the Plaintiff Class determines; (b) the Librarian and/or Deputy Librarian, at the option of the Plaintiffs' representatives; (c) Plaintiffs' Counsel; and (d) counsel for the Library.

VI.   ACCESS TO RECORDS

8.   The Library will maintain and make the agency records described in Paragraphs 9 and 10 below available to Plaintiffs' Counsel quarterly under the terms and conditions set forth in this Section. These records shall be used for the sole purpose

- 9 -

28

of assessing the Library's compliance with the terms of this
Agreement.

9.   Upon Preliminary Court Approval of this Agreement, the
Library shall maintain the following data regarding each and
every selection made under the new competitive selection process
for Professional and Administrative positions, in addition to the
recordkeeping requirements of the Uniform Guidelines: job title,
number of applicants, names of applicants, race of applicants (if
known), number of applicants meeting minimum qualifications,
number of applicants placed on a "better qualified" list (by race
if known), names of applicants referred to a rating panel and
placed on a "better qualified" list, number of applicants
interviewed by a selecting official (by race if known), names of
applicants interviewed by a selecting official, and name and race
of the person selected for each position.

10. Upon Preliminary Court Approval of this Agreement, the
Library shall maintain the following data regarding each and
every promotion made under the non-competitive selection system
in or into Professional and Administrative positions:

A.   For career ladder promotions: new grade level,
former grade level, name, race, and time-in-grade of person
promoted.

B.   For reclassifications resulting in a higher grade
level: new grade level, former grade level, name and race of
person affected by the reclassification, and salary increase of
the position reclassified.

- 10 -

29

C. For details to higher-graded positions lasting longer than 30 days: job title detailed to, job title detailed from, name and race of person detailed, duration of detail, and salary increase resulting from the detail.

D. For actions taken pursuant to Library of Congress Regulation 2010-14, section 4(a), resulting in selections in or into Professional and Administrative positions: name, race, current job, and salary increase of person being promoted; job title and known promotion potential of new position.

E. For actions taken pursuant to Library of Congress Regulation 2010-14, sections 4(E), 4(G), and 4(H), and repeat or consecutive actions pursuant to section 4(B): new grade level and job title; former grade level and job title; name, race and time-in-grade of appointees; salary differential, if any.

VII. MONETARY RELIEF

11. Upon Final Court Approval, Defendant shall pay to the Plaintiff Class the total sum of $8,500,000.00 in full and complete satisfaction of all claims for back pay arising out of the amended complaint filed in this action. The payment of this sum shall resolve all claims for monetary relief that are or could have been claimed in actions barred by the preclusive effect of this Agreement as provided in Paragraph 31, except for claims for attorneys' fees, costs and interest on fees and costs. This sum includes the amount the District Court awarded as monetary relief for members of the 4(a) Subclass. This sum is

- 11 -

30

subject to all appropriate deductions, including federal and
state taxes as well as retirement contributions. Defendant shall
be responsible for the payment of the employer's portion required
by law to be made with respect to such awards. It shall be
distributed pursuant to the formula set forth in Appendix C.

VIII. PROMOTIONS

    12. Within 90 days of Final Court Approval of this
Agreement, the Library shall promote 40 Class Members under the
terms and conditions provided in this paragraph. A
representative committee of the Plaintiff Class, to be appointed
by Plaintiffs' Counsel after consultation with Class Members,
shall identify the 40 Class Members to be promoted, no more than
ten of whom shall be retirees.

        A.   In the case of Class Members employed at the
Library at the time of Final Court Approval, the promotions under
this paragraph shall be to the next grade level in the Class
Member's promotion plan and the Class Member's duties and
responsibilities shall change in accordance with the existing
promotion plan. If, however, the Class Member has reached the
top grade in his or her promotion plan, he or she shall be
promoted to the next grade level in the General Schedule on an
incumbency basis in which he or she retains the same job with the
same duties and responsibilities. In both cases, the Class

- 12 -

31

Member will receive an increase in prospective pay plus time-in-grade credit for the higher-level grade.

B. In the case of Class Members who have retired prior to Final Court Approval, the Library shall promote each Class Member retroactively for a period of three years prior to his or her date of retirement. Appropriate contributions by the Defendant and the Class Member shall be made to the Class Member's retirement account. Any increase in annuity shall be prospective only.

C. Nothing in this paragraph shall be construed as expanding or reducing the total monetary settlement of $8.5 million described in paragraph 11 above, except to the extent of Defendant's payments of the government's share of retirement contributions to Class Members' accounts. Receipt of a promotion pursuant to this paragraph does not preclude any other relief, including back-pay and/or reassignment, which an individual may receive under this Agreement, nor does it obligate Defendant to pay any back pay or retroactive annuity payments in addition to the sum set forth in paragraph 11. No person shall receive more than one promotion and none of the promotions shall be into the Senior or Executive Levels.

D. The promotions provided in this Section are not intended to indicate that only a certain number of Class Members was capable or competent to perform work at a higher level at the Library before or during the pendency of this litigation.

- 13 -

32

IX. REASSIGNMENTS

13. Upon Final Court Approval of this Agreement, the
Library shall laterally reassign up to 10 Class Members under the
terms and conditions provided in this paragraph. The Library
shall provide to a representative committee of the Plaintiff
Class, to be appointed by Plaintiffs' Counsel after consultation
with Class Members, a list of positions which are open for
reassignment pursuant to this Paragraph. The representative
committee shall identify one Class Member to be reassigned to
each of ten positions to a maximum of 10 reassignments. The
Library shall have final approval of the positions to be offered
to each of the ten Class Members, each of whom shall have the
option of accepting the position offered or of requesting a
lateral reassignment to a different position. The Library,
however, shall not be obligated to transfer any Class Member into
a position that the Library determines would not be in the
interest of the Library or into which the Class Member is not
qualified, nor is any Class Member obligated to accept a
reassignment under this Paragraph. No Class Member may receive
more than one reassignment under the terms of this Agreement. If
a Class Member on the list prepared by the representative
committee chooses not to accept any reassignment, then another
Class Member shall be offered a reassignment pursuant to this
Paragraph. It is the intention of the parties that this Section
shall result in a total of ten reassignments being made, provided
that up to ten Plaintiffs elect to accept such reassignments.

- 14 -

Receipt of a reassignment pursuant to this paragraph does not preclude any other relief, including back-pay and/or promotion, which an individual may receive under this Agreement, nor does it obligate Defendant to pay any back pay or retroactive annuity payments in addition to the sum set forth in Paragraph 11.

X. INDEPENDENT REVIEW OF COMPETITIVE SELECTIONS

14. Upon Preliminary Court Approval, the Library shall, in consultation with Plaintiffs' Counsel, contract with the Office of Personnel Management ("OPM") to conduct a review of the Library's competitive selections to Professional and Administrative positions as of the one-year anniversary of the Effective Date of this Agreement. This review shall begin within thirty (30) days from the first anniversary of the Effective Date of this Agreement and shall be completed within ninety (90) days from the first anniversary of the Effective Date of this Agreement. In completing its review, OPM shall rely on the Uniform Guidelines and the provisions of this Agreement. If OPM determines that there has been a disparate impact on African-Americans under the Library's selection system, then OPM, Plaintiffs' Counsel and the Library shall analyze the reasons for the disparate impact, and the Library shall take appropriate corrective action in conformance with the Uniform Guidelines.

15. The Defendant shall pay the fees of OPM for the review contemplated by this Section.

- 15 -

34

XI. <u>TERM OF AGREEMENT AND ENFORCEMENT</u>

16. This Settlement Agreement and all provisions thereof will expire and shall be without force and effect four years from Final Court Approval. Notwithstanding the expiration of this Agreement, competitive selections made pursuant to Section II, non-competitive selections made pursuant to Section III, monetary relief awarded pursuant to Section VII, promotions made pursuant to Section VIII, and reassignments made pursuant to Section IX shall survive the expiration of the Agreement.

17. The District Court shall retain jurisdiction of this action solely for the purpose of addressing the parties' compliance with the provisions of this Settlement Agreement during the four-year period set forth in Paragraph 16 above.

XII. PROCEDURES FOR DETERMINING CLASS COMPOSITION
AND DISTRIBUTION OF MONETARY RELIEF

18. Within 60 days after Preliminary Court Approval of this Agreement, the Library shall disseminate a Notice to potential Class Members. In order to advise all potential Class Members of their rights under this Agreement, including Class Members who have retired, who have relocated, or whose current location is unknown, the Library shall arrange for the publication, at the Library's expense, of a Notice in the general news sections of The Washington Post, the Washington Times, the Washington D.C. Afro-American, the Library of Congress Gazette, the Montgomery County Journal, the Prince William County Journal, the Fairfax Journal, the Arlington Journal, and the Library of Congress

- 16 -

Information Bulletin on at least two occasions, two weeks apart.
The Notice shall also be mailed to all potential Class Members of
whom the Library is aware or who can be reasonably identified.
The contents of the Notices shall be subject to approval by the
Court. The proposed Notice for publication is attached hereto as
Appendix D, which is incorporated herein by reference. The
proposed Notice for mailing is attached hereto as Appendix E,
which is incorporated herein by reference.

19. The Notices referred to in paragraph 18 shall advise
all potential Class Members of: the background of the Agreement;
the general terms of the Agreement; and the application process
for potential Class Members who claim eligibility for relief.
The Notices shall also advise all potential Class Members that
they must respond by a specified date that shall be not less than
45 days from the date that notices are mailed to all potential
Class Members pursuant to Paragraph 18.

20. Within 30 days after Preliminary Court Approval,
Plaintiffs' Counsel, following consultation with Class Members,
shall appoint a Plaintiffs' Committee of up to 13 members to
decide, by simple majority, all issues of class membership and
allocation or distribution of the relief provided in this
Agreement. The members of this Plaintiffs' Committee shall be
given a reasonable amount of administrative leave with pay, if
currently employed at the Library of Congress, as is necessary to
perform all functions required by their membership on the
Plaintiffs' Committee. The Plaintiffs' Committee may confer with

- 17 -

36

Plaintiffs' Counsel in performing any or all of its functions.
Within 60 days after the deadline for responses to the Notice
described in Paragraph 19 above, the Plaintiffs' Committee shall
file a final report with the Court and distribute such report to
the class in accordance with Paragraph 23, below, which report
shall also be served on counsel for all parties. The report
shall include the particular qualifications for class membership
established by the Plaintiffs' Committee, the names and addresses
of Class Members as proposed by the Plaintiffs' Committee, the
names of individuals rejected for class membership, the reasons
for rejection for each individual, the individual distribution to
each Class Member as proposed by the Plaintiffs' Committee,
calculated pursuant to the formula set forth in Appendix C, and
the Class Members who will receive relief under Paragraphs 12 and
13. Any written waiver or settlement waiving prior claims signed
by a Class Member shall be provided to the Plaintiffs' Committee
by Defendant after the Plaintiffs' Committee has provided the
Library with a tentative list of Class Members, and such written
waiver or settlement shall be given effect by the Plaintiffs'
Committee in accordance with the terms of that written document.

21. All decisions of the Plaintiffs' Committee shall be
subject to review by the District Court as a part of the Fairness
Hearing conducted pursuant to Fed. R. Civ. P. 26(e). Defendant
shall not be responsible for determining individual membership in
the Plaintiff Class or resolving individual disputes arising from

- 18 -

37

claims regarding class membership or the amount of individual distributions of back pay.

XIII. PROCEDURES FOR FAIRNESS HEARING

22. The parties request that the Court schedule a Fairness Hearing pursuant to Fed. R. Civ. P. 23(e) to be held not earlier than 60 days after the submission of the final report by the Plaintiffs' Committee. Appendix F hereto is a proposed "Notice of Fairness Hearing on Settlement Proposal" ("Fairness Notice"), which the parties hereby request that the Court approve in connection with scheduling the Fairness Hearing.

23. Within 10 business days after receipt of the final report containing the proposed class list described in Paragraph 20 above and the individual notices regarding the distribution of awards described in Paragraph 20 above, the Library shall mail to all Class Members listed by the Plaintiffs' Committee and all persons rejected for class membership by the Plaintiffs' Committee a copy of the Fairness Notice together with a copy of this Agreement, all attachments to the Agreement, individual notice for the distribution of back pay described in Appendix C, and notice of Class Members receiving relief under Paragraphs 12 and 13. The Fairness Notice, without the above-described enclosures, shall also be posted in various public locations within the Library and published in the Library of Congress Gazette.

- 19 -

24. Any person who wishes to object to the terms of this Agreement, including any individual who challenges the Plaintiffs' Committee's determination regarding his or her class membership, calculation of an award of back pay, or distribution of other relief will be required, not less than 20 days prior to the Fairness Hearing, to submit a written statement to the Court, with copies to counsel for the parties. The statement shall contain the individual's name, address, and telephone number, along with a statement of his or her objection(s) to the Agreement and the reason(s) for the objection(s). Individuals who live more than fifty (50) miles from the District of Columbia and who make a challenge under this Paragraph shall not be required to appear at the Fairness Hearing.

25. Counsel For The Parties shall jointly use their best efforts to obtain prompt judicial approval of this Agreement. If the Court does not enter this Agreement as written after conducting the Fairness Hearing, the Agreement shall be voidable in its entirety at the option of either Plaintiffs or Defendant.

26. Following Final Court Approval of this Agreement, the Defendant shall take the necessary steps to have payment of the entire monetary relief set forth at Paragraph 11 processed through the General Accounting Office and to have individual checks made payable to Class Members in the amounts determined by the Plaintiffs' Committee, less appropriate deductions. Upon receipt of the checks, the Library shall distribute them, at Library expense, to each eligible class member in sealed

- 20 -

envelopes by delivery on the worksite or by certified mail return receipt requested. Prior to delivery of the checks, Plaintiffs' Counsel shall verify that the amount of money to be delivered to each class member is accurate.

XIV. OTHER MATTERS

27. Nothing in this Agreement may be taken as modifying either the statutory or regulatory procedures pertaining to initiating and maintaining administrative and judicial proceedings under Title VII of the Civil Rights Act of 1964, as amended, 42 U.S.C. §§ 2000e-16 et seq., or the federal civil service laws, or the requirement to exhaust administrative remedies prior to initiating suit under those statutes.

28. The parties to this action have entered into this Agreement as a compromise measure to terminate this action and resolve all issues in controversy between them. In recognition of this fact, neither the terms of this Agreement nor their substance may be offered, taken, construed, or introduced as evidence of liability or as an admission or statement of wrongdoing by the Defendant, either in this action or in any subsequent proceeding of any nature.

29. This Agreement, including all Appendices attached hereto, comprises the full and exclusive agreement of the parties with respect to the matters discussed herein. No representations or inducements to compromise this action or the administrative proceedings that gave rise to it have been made, other than those

recited in this Agreement. No statements other than those recited in this Agreement are binding upon the parties with respect to the disposition of this action or the administrative proceedings that gave rise to it.

30. The Plaintiffs, through Plaintiffs' Counsel, shall provide no less than 30 days notice to the Library's Office of the General Counsel of any alleged violation of the terms of this Agreement before seeking relief from any court or any administrative body outside the Library. The parties shall use their best efforts to resolve any claim of a violation of the Agreement, including the Library responding to any such notice within ten business days, explaining why the Library believes that the alleged violation does not violate the Agreement. This provision is not intended to, nor does it, confer jurisdiction to enforce this Agreement on any judicial or quasi-judicial body other than the District Court as provided in Paragraph 17 above.

31. The terms of this Agreement shall constitute full and complete satisfaction of all claims of Class Members against the defendant concerning racial discrimination in violation of Title VII of the Civil Rights Act of 1964, as amended, resulting in non-selection, either competitively or non-competitively, in or into Professional and Administrative positions within the Library that arise out of events occurring up to final District Court approval of the Agreement. Upon Final Court Approval of this Agreement, the class as a whole and each Class Member shall be

bound by the doctrines of res judicata and collateral estoppel with respect to all such claims.

32. No retaliation shall be taken against any class member because of his or her participation in this litigation. Subject to the 30-day notice provision in Paragraph 30 above, any class member claiming retaliation because of his or her participation in this litigation shall have the option of seeking relief from the District Court pursuant to the Court's continuing jurisdiction over this Agreement or pursuing a remedy under any other procedure established by law or regulation.

XV. REVIEW BY PLAINTIFFS' COUNSEL

33. This Agreement provides that certain selection and other procedures and certain rules and regulations shall be subject to review by Plaintiffs' Counsel. Such review is for the purpose of overseeing compliance with this Agreement. When conducting this review, Plaintiffs' Counsel shall be entitled to designate from time to time one or more expert consultants or other persons who shall assist Plaintiffs' Counsel in this review. Such persons, acting under the authority of Plaintiffs' Counsel, shall be authorized to review Library Human Resource Directives and other Library rules and regulations relevant to employee selection for Professional and Administrative positions, including, but not limited to, those set forth in this Agreement and issued pursuant to this Agreement, and any changes or modifications thereto made during the term of this Agreement.

- 23 -

34. The Library shall pay to Plaintiffs' Counsel their actual costs and expenses up to $15,000 per year for their use in paying reasonable expert fees and/or consultant fees. Plaintiffs' Counsel shall produce documentation in support of their request itemizing the services performed, the hours spent on those services, and the specific costs incurred. If Plaintiffs' Counsel do not spend the $15,000 in any given year, the unspent money shall not be carried over to any following year.

XVI. ATTORNEYS' FEES

35. After Final Court Approval of this Agreement, Defendant shall pay to Arent Fox Kintner Plotkin & Kahn the total sum of $1,646,119.67 for all attorneys' fees and expenses incurred by Plaintiffs through December 31, 1993. This amount includes all attorneys' fees and expenses due any legal representative of Plaintiffs and/or any Class Member. Distribution of the above fees and expenses shall be the responsibility of Arent Fox Kintner Plotkin & Kahn but shall be distributed by Arent Fox Kintner Plotkin & Kahn pursuant to the schedule of fees attached as Appendix G and incorporated herein which has been agreed to by Counsel for the Parties. The Plaintiffs reserve the right to seek interest on the attorneys' fees and expenses agreed upon in this paragraph in the event that the Supreme Court finds that the Civil Rights Act of 1991 applies to cases pending at the time of enactment of that statute. In the event the Plaintiffs are

- 24 -

43

entitled to interest, but the parties are unable to resolve the amount of interest to be paid, the parties may petition the Court.

36. Thereafter, until the expiration of this Agreement, Defendant shall pay reasonable attorneys' fees plus costs as provided by law for services performed in connection with matters arising under this Agreement. With respect to these attorneys' fees and costs, Plaintiffs' Counsel shall produce documentation in support of their request itemizing the services performed, the hours spent on those services, and the specific costs incurred. Defendant shall not be obligated to pay attorneys' fees and/or costs for any court action alleging a violation of this Agreement or alleging retaliation pursuant to paragraph 32 unless the Plaintiffs are the prevailing party.

37. The parties shall attempt in good faith to resolve any disputes concerning attorneys' fees and costs. Any dispute that cannot be resolved may be submitted to the Court.

(signature)

MARC L. FLEISCHAKER
D.C. Bar #4333
DAVID L. KELLEHER
D.C. Bar #388661
MINDY L. KLASKY
D.C. Bar #426589
Arent Fox Kintner
   Plotkin & Kahn
1050 Connecticut Ave., N.W.
Washington, D.C. 20036
(202) 857-6000

(signature)

JOSEPH M. SELLERS
D.C. Bar #318410
AVIS E. BUCHANAN
D.C. Bar #365208
Washington Lawyers
   Committee for Civil
   Rights and
   Urban Affairs
1300 Nineteenth St. N.W.
Suite 500
Washington, D.C. 20036
(202) 835-0031

Counsel for Plaintiffs

(signature)

ERIC H. HOLDER, JR.
D.C. Bar # 303115
United States Attorney

(signature)

JOHN D. BATES
D.C. Bar #934327
Assistant United States Attorney

(signature)

JOHN OLIVER BIRCH
D.C. Bar # 234419
Assistant United States Attorney

(signature)

MADELYN E. JOHNSON
D.C. Bar #292318
Assistant United States Attorney
555 4th Street, N.W.
10th Floor
Washington, D.C. 20001
(202) 514-7135

(signature)

LANA KAY JONES
D.C. Bar #929089
Associate General Counsel
Library of Congress
Washington, D.C. 20540
(202) 707-6316

Counsel for Defendant

SO ORDERED: _____

               UNITED STATES DISTRICT JUDGE

    Date: _____, 1994

- 26 -

45

SERIES NUMBER	SERIES TITLE
0019	Safety Technician
0021	Community Planning Technician
0025	Park Ranger (GS 1-4)
0026	Park Technician
0029	Environmental Protection Assistant
0072	Fingerprint Identification (GS 7-10)
0090	Guide
0102	Social Science Aid & Technician
0119	Economics Assistant
0181	Psychology Aid and Technician
0186	Social Services Aid and Assistant
0189	Recreation Aid & Assistant
0203	Personnel Clerical and Assistance (GS 6 and above)
0204	Military Personnel Clerical and Technician (GS 7 and above)
0301	General Clerical and Administrative (GS 7-10)
0303	Miscellaneous Clerk and Assistant (GS 6 and above.)
0326	Office Automation Clerical and Assistance (GS 5 and above)
0332	Computer Operation
0335	Computer Clerk and Assistant (GS 5 and above)
0344	Management and Program Clerical Assistant (GS 6 and above)
0361	Equal Opportunity Assistance
0362	Electric Accounting Machine Project Planner
0388	Cryptographic Equipment Operation
0389	Radio Operating
0390	Telecommunications Processing
0392	General Telecommunications
0393	Communications Specialist
0404	Biological Science Technician
0421	Plant Protection Technician
0455	Range Technician
0456	Forest and Range Fire Control
0458	Soil Conservation Technician
0459	Irrigation System Operation
0462	Forestry Technician
0501	General Accounting Clerk & Administrative (GS 7-10)
0503	Financial Clerical and Assistance (GS 6 and above)
0520	Accounts Maintenance Clerical (GS 4 and above)
O525	Accounting Technician (GS 4 and above)

APPENDIX A

46

SERIES NUMBER	SERIES TITLE
0526	Tax Technician
0541	Fiscal Auditing
0544	Civilian Pay (GS 5 and above)
0545	Military Pay (GS 5 and above)
0561	Budget Clerical and Assistance (GS 6 and above)
0592	Tax Examining (GS 6 and above)
0593	Insurance Accounts
0620	Practical Nurse
0621	Nursing Assistant
0622	Medical Supply Aide and Technician
0625	Autopsy Assistant
0636	Rehabilitation Therapy Assistant
0640	Health Aid and Technician
0642	Nuclear Medicine Technician
0645	Medical Medicine Technician
0646	Pathology Technician
0647	Diagnostic Radiologic Technologist
0648	Therapeutic Radiologic Technician
0649	Medical Instrument Technician
0650	Medical Technical Assistant
0651	Respiratory Therapist
0661	Pharmacy Technician
0664	Restoration Technician
0667	Orthotist and Prosthetist
0669	Medical Records Administration
0672	Prosthetic Representative
0675	Medical Records Technician
0681	Dental Assistant
0682	Dental Hygiene
0683	Dental Laboratory Aid and Technician
0684	Public Health Dental Hygiene
0698	Environmental Health Technician
0699	Medical and Health Student Trainee
0704	Animal Health Technician
0802	Engineering Technician
0805	Engineering Technology
0809	Construction Control
0817	Surveying Technician

SERIES NUMBER	SERIES TITLE
0818	Engineering Drafting
0856	Electronics Technician
0895	Industrial Engineering Technician
0962	Contact Representative
0963	Legal Instruments Examining (GS 6 and above)
0986	Legal Clerical and Assistance (GS 7 and above)
0990	General Claims Examining (GS 1-10)
0991	Workman Comp Claims Examining
0992	Loss and Damage Claims Examining
0993	Social Insurance Claims Examining
0994	Unemployment Compensation Claims Examining
0995	Dependents and Estates Claims Examining
0996	Veterans Claims Examining
0997	Civil Service Retirement Claims Examining
1001	General Arts and Information (GS 7-10)
1010	Exhibits Specialist
1016	Museum Specialist and Technician
1020	Illustrating
1060	Photography
1087	Editorial Assistance (GS 6 and above)
1101	General Business and Industry (GS 6-10)
1105	Purchasing
1106	Procurement Clerical and Technician (GS 6 and above)
1107	Property Disposal Clerical and Technician (GS 6 and above)
1152	Production Control
1202	Patent Technician
1211	Copyright Technician
1311	Physical Science Technician
1316	Hydrologic Technician
1341	Meteorological Technician
1371	Cartographic Technician
1374	Geodetic Technician
1411	Library Technician
1421	Archives Technician (GS 7 and above)
1521	Mathematics Technician
1531	Statistical Assistant (GS 7-10)
1541	Cryptanalysis
1641	Buildings and Grounds Technical Management

SERIES NUMBER	SERIES TITLE
1670	Equipment Specialist (GS 1-10)
1702	Education and Training Technician
1802	Compliance Inspection and Support (GS 6 and above)
1820	Safety Inspection
1855	Alcohol Tax Technician
1860	Public Health Inspection
1862	Consumer Safety Inspection
1863	Food Inspection
1895	Customs Warehouse Officer
1897	Customs Aid (GS 7 and above)
1899	Investigation Student Trainee (GS 7-10)
1960	Quality Inspection
1980	Agricultural Commodity Grading
1981	Agricultural Commodity Aid
2001	General Supply (GS 7-10)
2005	Supply Clerical and Technician (GS 7 and above)
2101	General Transportation
2102	Transportation Clerk and Assistant (GS 6 and above)
2111	Transportation Rate and Tariff Examining (GS 6 and above)
2131	Freight Rate (GS 7 and above)
2133	Passenger Rate (GS 7 and above)
2135	Transportation Loss & Damage Claims Examining
2144	Cargo Scheduling
2154	Air Traffic Assistance
2181	Aircraft Operation
2183	Air Navigation
2185	Aircrew Technician

SERIES NUMBER	SERIES TITLE
0525	Accounting Technician (GS 4 and above)
0520	Accounts Maintenance Clerical (GS 4 and above)
1981	Agricultural Commodity Aid
1980	Agricultural Commodity Grading
2183	Air Navigation
2154	Air Traffic Assistance
2181	Aircraft Operation
2185	Aircrew Technician
1855	Alcohol Tax Technician
0704	Animal Health Technician
1421	Archives Technician (GS 7 and above)
0625	Autopsy Assistant
0404	Biological Science Technician
0561	Budget Clerical and Assistance (GS 6 and above)
1641	Buildings and Grounds Technical Management
2144	Cargo Scheduling
1371	Cartographic Technician
0997	Civil Service Retirement Claims Examining
0544	Civilian Pay (GS 5 and above)
0393	Communications Specialist
0021	Community Planning Technician
1802	Compliance Inspection and Support (GS 6 and above)
0335	Computer Clerk and Assistant (GS 5 and above)
0332	Computer Operation
0809	Construction Control
1862	Consumer Safety Inspection
0962	Contact Representative
1211	Copyright Technician
1541	Cryptanalysis
0388	Cryptographic Equipment Operation
1897	Customs Aid (GS 7 and above)
1895	Customs Warehouse Officer
0681	Dental Assistant
0682	Dental Hygiene
0683	Dental Laboratory Aid and Technician
0995	Dependents and Estates Claims Examining
0647	Diagnostic Radiologic Technologist
0119	Economics Assistant

50

SERIES NUMBER	SERIES TITLE
1087	Editorial Assistance (GS 6 and above)
1702	Education and Training Technician
0362	Electric Accounting Machine Project Planner
0856	Electronics Technician
0818	Engineering Drafting
0802	Engineering Technician
0805	Engineering Technology
0698	Environmental Health Technician
0029	Environmental Protection Assistant
0361	Equal Opportunity Assistance
1670	Equipment Specialist (GS 1-10)
1010	Exhibits Specialist
0503	Financial Clerical and Assistance (GS 6 and above)
0072	Fingerprint Identification (GS 7-10)
0541	Fiscal Auditing
1863	Food Inspection
0456	Forest and Range Fire Control
0462	Forestry Technician
2131	Freight Rate (GS 7 and above)
0501	General Accounting Clerk & Administrative (GS 7-10)
1001	General Arts and Information (GS 7-10)
1101	General Business and Industry (GS 6-10)
0990	General Claims Examining (GS 1-10)
0301	General Clerical and Administrative (GS 7-10)
2001	General Supply (GS 7-10)
0392	General Telecommunications
2101	General Transportation
1374	Geodetic Technician
0090	Guide
0640	Health Aid and Technician
1316	Hydrologic Technician
1020	Illustrating
0895	Industrial Engineering Technician
0593	Insurance Accounts
1899	Investigation Student Trainee (GS 7-10)
0459	Irrigation System Operation
0986	Legal Clerical and Assistance (GS 7 and above)
0963	Legal Instruments Examining (GS 6 and above)

51

**SERIES
NUMBER**   **SERIES TITLE**

1411   Library Technician
0992   Loss and Damage Claims Examining
0344   Management and Program Clerical Assistant (GS 6 and above)
1521   Mathematics Technician
0699   Medical and Health Student Trainee
0649   Medical Instrument Technician
0669   Medical Records Administration
0675   Medical Records Technician
0622   Medical Supply Aide and Technician
0650   Medical Technical Assistant
1341   Meteorological Technician
0545   Military Pay (GS 5 and above)
0204   Military Personnel Clerical and Technician (GS 7 and above)
0303   Miscellaneous Clerk and Assistant (GS 6 and above.)
1016   Museum Specialist and Technician
0645   Medical Medicine Technician
0642   Nuclear Medicine Technician
0621   Nursing Assistant
0326   Office Automation Clerical and Assistance (GS 5 and above)
0667   Orthotist and Prosthetist
0025   Park Ranger (GS 1-4)
0026   Park Technician
2133   Passenger Rate (GS 7 and above)
1202   Patent Technician
0646   Pathology Technician
0203   Personnel Clerical and Assistance (GS 6 and above)
0661   Pharmacy Technician
1060   Photography
1311   Physical Science Technician
0421   Plant Protection Technician
0620   Practical Nurse
1106   Procurement Clerical and Technician (GS 6 and above)
1152   Production Control
1107   Property Disposal Clerical and Technician (GS 6 and above)
0672   Prosthetic Representative
0181   Psychology Aid and Technician
0684   Public Health Dental Hygiene
1860   Public Health Inspection

52

SERIES NUMBER	SERIES TITLE
1105	Purchasing
1960	Quality Inspection
0389	Radio Operating
0455	Range Technician
0189	Recreation Aid & Assistant
0636	Rehabilitation Therapy Assistant
0651	Respiratory Therapist
0664	Restoration Technician
1820	Safety Inspection
0019	Safety Technician
0993	Social Insurance Claims Examining
0102	Social Science Aid & Technician
0186	Social Services Aid and Assistant
0458	Soil Conservation Technician
1531	Statistical Assistant (GS 7-10)
2005	Supply Clerical and Technician (GS 7 and above)
0817	Surveying Technician
0592	Tax Examining (GS 6 and above)
0526	Tax Technician
0390	Telecommunications Processing
0648	Therapeutic Radiologic Technician
2102	Transportation Clerk and Assistant (GS 6 and above)
2135	Transportation Loss & Damage Claims Examining
2111	Transportation Rate and Tariff Examining (GS 6 and above)
0994	Unemployment Compensation Claims Examining
0996	Veterans Claims Examining
0991	Workman Comp Claims Examining

FILLING VACANCIES UNDER THE LIBRARY'S REVISED COMPETITIVE SELECTION PROCESS

STEP 1:   PREPARATION FOR POSTING

1. Service Unit determines need/gets fiscal approval to post position.

2. The supervisor of the position reviews and certifies the position description for accuracy and completeness, consulting incumbents as appropriate. A position cannot be filled without a certification of position description accuracy and completeness. If the supervisor determines through this review that the position description is not accurate, he/she prepares a revised position description. If the Human Resources Directorate determines that the changes are substantial, the new or revised position description is subject to a classification review.

3. Service Unit prepares a request for vacancy announcement and forwards this document, along with the position description and relevant background material (organizational chart, mission and functional statements, etc.) to the Human Resources Directorate.

4. The Human Resources Directorate reviews the submitted package and designates a diverse group of individuals to serve as Subject Matter Experts (SMEs). SMEs are individuals who have performed or are very knowledgeable of the responsibilities of the position being filled, and who are at or above the grade level of the position. Applicants for the position to be filled, as well as the selecting official, cannot serve as SMEs for that position. Human Resources designates three or more subject matter experts for each panel, depending on the number of incumbents in the position under analysis. Incumbents shall be fairly represented on each panel of experts, and in no instance shall there be less than one incumbent subject matter expert, unless there is in fact no incumbent, or all incumbents decline to serve. As appropriate, additional individuals who have knowledge of the work behaviors of the position may be asked to provide technical assistance to the subject matter experts. Human Resource Specialists/Consultants direct the job analysis effort.

5. Job analysis is conducted in accordance with the Uniform Guidelines on Employee Selection Procedures and the Human Resources Directorate's Standard Operating Procedures for Job Analysis to perform the following tasks:

    a. Identify the major duties, relying to the greatest extent possible on observable work behaviors or tasks of the position. The panel utilizes various tools, including but not limited to: their knowledge of the position under review or like positions; the position description of record, OPM qualification standards, and relevant occupational literature;

b.   Identify the knowledge, skills and abilities ("KSAs") required to perform the duties of the position;

c.   Analyze the KSAs to determine those appropriate for use as evaluation criteria -- as minimum qualification requirements, quality ranking factors, or both;

d.   Develop a written rating instrument (crediting plan) which includes quality ranking factors which have been identified as indicators of successful performance in the position; operational definitions for each KSA; task examples for three levels of proficiency; and general level definitions for three levels of proficiency. Unit weighting of KSAs is used, unless other weighting methods are strongly supported by the job analysis.

6.   Following certification of all documents, the Human Resources Directorate drafts the vacancy announcement. All job analysis packages for professional and administrative positions are reviewed by the Affirmative Action/Special Programs Office to ensure that requirements are not present which would arbitrarily or inadvertently exclude minorities, women and persons with disabilities.

STEP 2: VACANCY ANNOUNCEMENT IS POSTED/APPLICATIONS ARE RECEIVED

1.   Prior to closing of vacancies for professional and administrative positions, an affirmative action review is conducted to determine whether the initial applicant pool is diverse. A decision is then made as to whether the posting should be closed or extended, to widen the area of consideration.

STEP 3: APPLICATIONS ARE RATED FOR MINIMUM QUALIFICATIONS

1.   Human Resources Specialists apply a "pass-fail" analysis to each minimum qualification for each applicant, relying exclusively on the information contained in the SF-171 and required attachments.

2.   An affirmative action review is conducted to determine whether the pool of candidates being referred to the rating panel is diverse. A decision is then made as to whether to proceed with the selection process.

2

1.   For positions at or above the GS-5 level[1], a rating panel is selected by the Human
       Resources Directorate. This panel is comprised of three of more subject matter
       experts at the same or higher grade level of the position being filled, and reflects
       the diversity of the Library's workforce.

2.   Rating panel members are provided instruction in the rating process and procedures
       prior to rating applications. At the start of each panel, an assigned Human
       Resources Specialist reviews the panel process, discusses the crediting plan in detail
       and reminds panel members of their duties and responsibilities during the entire
       process. The specialist remains with the panel to ensure that the crediting plan is
       understood, and is available to the panel throughout the rating process.

3.   The panel evaluates each candidate independently by analyzing his or her
       experience, education and training against the ranking factors, using the crediting
       plan established for the position. After each panel member has rated each
       candidate for each factor and totaled the results, the panel members present their
       rating sheets to the Human Resources Specialist.

4.   The Human Resources Specialist utilizes an appropriate statistical test to calculate
       interrater reliability. If the application of the rating guide is not found to be
       reliable, the selection process is curtailed until problems are identified and resolved.

5.   Once the application of the crediting plan is found to be reliable, the human
       resources specialist totals the panel members' scores for each candidate and ranks
       the candidates in numerical order. The specialist then determines the point in the
       numerical order above which all candidates will be included on the merit promotion
       certificate issued to the selecting official.

6.   Human Resources Specialists identify candidates to be referred to the selecting
       official by using Method 1 or Method 2 described below.

       Method 1:   A natural break is established as a cutoff point -- a dividing point
                   between the highly qualified and the qualified candidates. The cut-
                   off score will be determined based on a ranking of the candidates by
                   the total score received. The natural break is the point at which
                   scores reflect a meaningful distinction between the rated candidates.
                   Where multiple natural breaks occur, consideration is given to

---

[1]this includes all professional and administrative positions and many technical and
clerical positions

referring a reasonable number of candidates reflecting the diversity of the Library's workforce.

Method 2:   Where no natural break can be determined, all Qualified candidates (candidates whose rating equals or exceeds the total of all the KSAs at the Qualified Level) are referred.

7.   An affirmative action review is conducted to determine whether the pool of candidates being referred to the Selecting Official is diverse. A decision is then made as to whether to proceed with the selection process.

8.   The highly qualified list of candidates (or, in the instances where Method 2 is used, the qualified list of candidates) is referred to the selecting official. All referred applicants must be given the opportunity for an interview.

STEP 5:   APPLICANTS ARE INTERVIEWED

1.   Library Selecting Officials and Human Resources Specialists work together in preparing a standardized set of interview questions to be used for each selection opportunity. These questions must be directly related to the knowledge, skills, and abilities identified in the job analysis process and required to perform the job successfully.

2.   Selecting Officials are provided training in proper interviewing prior to conducting interviews.

3.   Selecting Officials conduct interviews, taking and retaining notes on each interview. These notes become part of the merit selection file.

4.   Selecting Officials, upon completion of the interview process and at the point of making a selection, must prepare written explanations for the selection and non-selection of each applicant interviewed. Should the Selecting Official indicate that he or she is unable to select any of the referred highly qualified candidates, the Service Unit is notified, and a determination made as to whether reposting is necessary. The Selecting Official forwards a Personnel Action Recommendation for the proposed selectee, along with interview notes and justifications, to the Human Resources Specialist.

STEP 6:   SELECTION DECISION MADE

1.   Selection recommendations, as well as the entire merit selection file, are reviewed by the Human Resources Service Unit for conformance with merit principles, Section 15C of the Uniform Guidelines, other Library regulations and affirmative

4

action goals.

2.   Affirmative Action reviews are conducted for all professional and administrative positions.

5

DISTRIBUTION FORMULA

The award of back pay shall be divided as follows:

I.   Following the distribution set forth at Paragraph IV below, the Plaintiffs' Committee shall distribute monetary relief to Class Members who submitted claims in the 4(a) portion of this case. Such distribution shall be $805,264.01. For purposes of making the back pay distribution, the Plaintiffs' Committee shall utilize each 4(a) Class Member's Notice of Claim form previously submitted. Each 4(a) Class Member shall be "assigned" to the highest grade appointment listed on his or her form which the Plaintiffs' Committee believes to be appropriate. Beginning and ending dates shall be calculated by the Plaintiffs' Committee for each 4(a) appointment, and, the total number of months shall be calculated for all appointments. The maximum number of months for any 4(a) appointment shall be 60. The back pay award shall be divided by the total number of months, yielding a Per Month Value for the 4(a) appointments. The Per Month Value shall be multiplied by the number of complete months each appointment lasted, yielding a Per Appointment Value. Each Per Appointment Value shall be divided by the number of claimants for that appointment, and the Plaintiffs' Committee shall distribute the resulting amount to each 4(a) Class Member who claimed for that appointment. In no event shall any 4(a) Claimant receive in excess of $20,000. If the award would otherwise exceed $20,000, the excess shall revert to the remaining 4(a) claimants on a per capita basis.

II. Following the distributions set forth at Paragraph I above and Paragraph IV below, fifty percent of the remaining award shall be allocated to those Class Members who were in Professional and Administrative positions. The second fifty percent of the remaining award shall be divided between those Class Members who were in Professional and Administrative positions and those Class Members who were not but who believe they would have been had there been objective, legal, and appropriate standards for entry into those positions. Such division shall be proportional to the number of Class Members in each group. This formula is illustrated by the examples set forth in the examples attached hereto, which are incorporated herein by reference.

III. Following the division of the total backpay award into one pool for Professional or Administrative employees and another pool for employees not in Professional or Administrative positions, as described in Paragraphs I and II above and Paragraph IV below, the Plaintiffs' Committee will add up the total complete months of service for each claimant who had been accepted as a Class Member. The totals will be calculated separately for each pool. The total number of months will then be divided into the total amount of the pool to be distributed (that is, after interest is added, bonuses are deducted, and 4(a) relief is deducted) to determine the amount per month which each claimant will receive. That amount will then be multiplied by the number of complete months the claimant was at the Library during the relevant time period. Six months will be deducted for every competitive promotion which the individual

- 2 -

actually received during the back pay period. Further examples are set forth in the attachment hereto.

IV. The Plaintiffs' Committee shall make the following awards in recognition of the time and energy which the following individuals have contributed to the Cook class actions: $25,000 to Howard Cook as class representative, $10,000 to Tommy Shaw as sub-class representative, $5,000 to each additional named plaintiff, and $1,000 to each intervenor.

- 3 -

61

EXAMPLES OF DISTRIBUTION FORMULA

Example 1:   There are 1,000 claimants who were in Professional and Administrative positions, and 1,000 claimants who were not in such positions. The total fund ($8.5 million plus interest, less Paragraph IV distributions, less previous payments made to 4(a) claimants) would then be divided with 75% going to those in Professional and Administrative positions and 25% going to those not in such positions.

Example 2:   There are 1,000 claimants who were in Professional and Administrative positions, and 500 claimants who were not in such positions. The total fund ($8.5 million plus interest, less Paragraph IV distributions, less previous payments made to 4(a) claimants) would then be divided with 87.5% going to those in Professional and Administrative positions, and 12.5% going to those not in such positions.

Example 3:   There are 1,000 claimants who were in Professional and Administrative positions, and 2,000 claimants who were not in such positions. The total fund ($8.5 million plus interest, less Paragraph IV distributions, less previous payments made to 4(a) claimants) would then be divided with 62.5% going to

- 4 -

those in Professional and Administrative positions, and 37.5% going to those not in such positions.

Example 4: Using the number of claimants as set forth in Example 1, and assuming the average claimant was at the Library of Congress for five years between November 25, 1975 and the date of Preliminary Court Approval (after the appropriate six-month deductions for competitive promotions):

Professional and Administrative

1,000 claimants x 60 months = 60,000 months

$8.5 million x 75% = $6,375,000

$6,375,000 ÷ 60,000 = $106.25 per month

(A claimant having served five years with no promotions would receive $6,375; a claimant having served 20 years with no promotions would receive $25,500.00)

Non-Professional and Administrative

1,000 claimants x 60 months = 60,000 months

$8.5 million x 25% = $2,125,000

$2,125,000 ÷ 60,000 = $35.42 per month

- 5 -

(A claimant having served five years with no promotions would receive $2,125.20; a claimant having served 20 years with no promotions would receive $8,500.80.)

Example 5: Using the number of claimants as set forth in Example 2, and assuming the average claimant was at the Library of Congress for five years between November 25, 1975 and the date of Preliminary Court Approval (after the appropriate six-month deductions for competitive promotions):

Professional and Administrative

1,000 claimants x 60 months = 60,000 months

$8.5 million x 87.5% = $7,437,500

$7,437,500 ÷ 60,000 = $123.96 per month

(A claimant having served five years with no promotions would receive $7,437.50; a claimant having served 20 years with no promotions would receive $29,750.40.)

Non-Professional and Administrative

500 claimants x 60 months = 30,000 months

$8.5 million x 12.5% = $1,062,500

$1,062,500 ÷ 30,000 = $35.42 per month

(Same result per claimant as in example 4.)

- 6 -

Example 6: Using the number of claimants as set forth in Example 3, and assuming the average claimant was at the Library of Congress for five years between November 25, 1975 and the date of Preliminary Court Approval (after the appropriate six-month deductions for competitive promotions):

Professional and Administrative
1,000 claimants x 60 months = 60,000 months
$8.5 million x 62.5% = $5,312,500
$5,312,500 ÷ 60,000 = $88.54 per month

(A claimant having served five years with no promotions would receive $5,312.40; a claimant having served 20 years with no promotions would receive $21,249.60.)

Non-Professional and Administrative
2,000 claimants x 60 months = 120,000 months
$8.5 million x 37.5% = $3,187,500
$3,187,500 ÷ 120,000 = $26.56 per month

(A claimant having served five years with no promotions would receive $1,593.60; a claimant having served 20 years with no promotions would receive $6,374.40.)

- 7 -

TO: All Past and Present Employees of the Library of Congress

A proposed settlement has been reached in an equal employment class action brought on behalf of African-American employees of the Library of Congress. The Complaint in this class action alleged racial discrimination in competitive and non-competitive promotions and personnel actions in or into professional and administrative jobs. The case is captioned Cook v. Billington, C.A. No. 82-0400 (NHJ/PJA). The plaintiff class certified by the District Court on December 13, 1988 is as follows:

> All past, present and future black employees at the Library of Congress who possess the minimum objective qualifications necessary to be eligible under valid, nondiscriminatory standards for selection or promotion to any professional or administrative position at the Library of Congress, and who have been, are being, or may in the future be, denied equal employment or promotional opportunities as a result of defendant's discriminatory practices complained of herein.

December 13, 1988 Opinion at 3. The plaintiff class also includes all members of the 4(a) Subclass certified by the Court on June 8, 1984 as:

> All past, present and future black employees at the Library of Congress ...
>
> * * *
>
> who were not promoted to positions by reason of the Library of Congress Regulations, section 4(a).

June 8, 1984 Opinion at 3-4. If you fall within either, or both, of the descriptions quoted above and you were employed by the

APPENDIX D

66

Library of Congress on or after November 25, 1975, this proposed settlement may affect you.

The proposed Settlement Agreement provides significant monetary relief as well as injunctive measures to ensure equity in promotions, competitive selections and other employment practices. The Agreement includes a provision for independent review of the Library's competitive selection process by the Office of Personnel Management and other monitors to insure that the process is fair and equitable. The Agreement will give representatives of the plaintiff class the opportunity to meet with the Librarian and/or Deputy Librarian at least twice annually throughout the duration of the Agreement. It also provides a limited number of promotions and career development opportunities for members of the class.

Questions regarding class membership and distribution of relief will be decided by a Committee composed of up to 13 class members. **IF YOU BELIEVE THAT YOU ARE A MEMBER OF THE CLASS DESCRIBED ABOVE, YOU MUST NOTIFY THE COMMITTEE BY SENDING YOUR NAME, HOME ADDRESS, HOME TELEPHONE NUMBER AND OFFICE TELEPHONE NUMBER TO THE FOLLOWING ADDRESS:**

> MARC L. FLEISCHAKER
> DAVID L. KELLEHER
> MINDY L. KLASKY
> Arent Fox Kintner
>   Plotkin & Kahn
> 1050 Connecticut Ave., N.W.
> Washington, D.C. 20036
> ATTENTION: COOK CLASS ACTION

YOUR NOTICE MUST BE RECEIVED BY _____, 1994.

N O T I C E

TO: All Past and Present Employees of the Library of Congress

A proposed settlement has been reached in an equal employment class action brought on behalf of African-American employees of the Library of Congress. The Complaint in this class action alleged racial discrimination in competitive and non-competitive promotions and personnel actions in or into professional and administrative jobs. The case is captioned <u>Cook v. Billington</u>, C.A. No. 82-0400 (NHJ/PJA). The plaintiff class certified by the District Court on December 13, 1988 is as follows:

> All past, present and future black employees at the Library of Congress who possess the minimum objective qualifications necessary to be eligible under valid, nondiscriminatory standards for selection or promotion to any professional or administrative position at the Library of Congress, and who have been, are being, or may in the future be, denied equal employment or promotional opportunities as a result of defendant's discriminatory practices complained of herein.

December 13, 1988 Opinion at 3. The plaintiff class also includes all members of the 4(a) Subclass certified by the Court on June 8, 1984 as:

> All past, present and future black employees at the Library of Congress ...
>
> * * *
>
> who were not promoted to positions by reason of the Library of Congress Regulations, section 4(a).

June 8, 1984 Opinion at 3-4. If you fall within either, or both, of the descriptions quoted above and you were employed by the

Library of Congress on or after November 25, 1975, this proposed settlement may affect you.

The proposed Settlement Agreement provides significant monetary relief as well as injunctive measures to ensure equity in promotions, competitive selections and other employment practices. The Agreement includes a provision for independent review of the Library's competitive selection process by the Office of Personnel Management and other monitors to insure that the process is fair and equitable. The Agreement will give representatives of the plaintiff class the opportunity to meet with the Librarian and/or Deputy Librarian at least twice annually throughout the duration of the Agreement. It also provides a limited number of promotion and career development opportunities for members of the class.

Questions regarding class membership and distribution of relief will be decided by a Committee composed of up to 13 class members. **IF YOU BELIEVE THAT YOU ARE A MEMBER OF THE CLASS DESCRIBED ABOVE, YOU MUST COMPLETE THE ATTACHED CLAIM FORM AND RETURN IT TO:**

> **MARC L. FLEISCHAKER**
> **DAVID L. KELLEHER**
> **MINDY L. KLASKY**
> **Arent Fox Kintner Plotkin &**
> **Kahn**
> **1050 Connecticut Ave., N.W.**
> **Washington, D.C. 20036**
> **ATTENTION: COOK CLASS ACTION**

YOUR CLAIM FORM MUST BE RECEIVED BY _____, 1994.

To: MARC L. FLEISCHAKER, ESQ.
Arent Fox Kintner Plotkin & Kahn
1050 Connecticut Avenue, N.W.
Washington, D.C. 20036-5339
ATTENTION: COOK CLASS ACTION

The undersigned declares that the following information is accurate
and true to the best of his/her knowledge:

1. Name: _____

2. Home address: _____

_____

3. Home telephone: _____

4. Work telephone: _____

5. Name while employed at Library of Congress (if different from
current name):

_____

6. Race: _____

7. Date employment began at Library of Congress:

_____

8. Name and series of first jŏb at Library of Congress:

_____

9. Date, name of job, and series of job for **each** competitive or
noncompetitive promotion received at Library of Congress (if any).
Please place a * by any promotion into a professional or
administrative position:[1]

_____

_____

_____

_____

---

[1] Please feel free to attach a sheet of paper with additional
information for any question, indicating which question you are
supplementing.

10. Name and series of last job at Library of Congress (or current job if still employed at Library of Congress)

_____

11. Date of last employment by Library of Congress:

_____

12. Do you want to be considered for a promotion under the Settlement Agreement? (Answer yes or no, and if yes, provide a brief explanation of why you should receive this extraordinary form of relief.)

_____

_____

_____

_____

_____

_____

13. Do you want to be considered for a reassignment under the Settlement Agreement? (Answer yes or no, and if yes, provide a brief explanation of why you should receive this extraordinary form of relief.)

_____

_____

_____

_____

_____

14. Please include any additional comments which you believe are necessary for the committee to make a decision about your relief under the Settlement Agreement.

_____

_____

_____

_____

For purposes of this class action, the Court has defined the class to be:

> All past, present and future black employees at the Library of Congress who possess the minimum objective qualifications necessary to be eligible under valid, nondiscriminatory standards for selection or promotion to any professional or administrative position at the Library of Congress, and who have been, are being, or may in the future be, denied equal employment or promotional opportunities as a result of defendant's discriminatory practices complained of herein.

By signing below, you indicate that you believe that you are a member of the class and that all the facts you have set forth in this Claim Form are true, to the best of your knowledge.

Signed: _____

Date: _____

72

Please feel free to use this sheet of paper or other sheets of paper to provide additional information for any question, indicating which question you are supplementing.

_____

_____

_____

_____

_____

_____

_____

_____

_____

_____

_____

_____

_____

_____

_____

_____

_____

_____

_____

_____

_____

_____

_____

_____

_____

UNITED STATES DISTRICT COURT
FOR THE DISTRICT OF COLUMBIA

HOWARD R.L. COOK, et al.,

  Plaintiffs,

      v.   C.A. No. 82-0400 (NHJ/PJA)

JAMES H. BILLINGTON,

  Defendant.

NOTICE OF FAIRNESS HEARING ON PROPOSED SETTLEMENT

TO: All Past and Present Employees of the Library of Congress

    A proposed settlement has been reached in an equal
employment class action brought on behalf of African-American
employees of the Library of Congress who fit within the
definition of the plaintiff class certified by United States
District Judge Norma H. Johnson. The case is captioned Cook v.
Billington, C.A. No. 82-0400 (NHJ/PJA). The plaintiff class
certified by the District Court on December 13, 1988 is as
follows:

> All past, present and future black employees
> at the Library of Congress who possess the
> minimum objective qualifications necessary to
> be eligible under valid, nondiscriminatory
> standards for selection or promotion to any
> professional or administrative position at
> the Library of Congress, and who have been,
> are being, or may in the future be, denied
> equal employment or promotional opportunities
> as a result of defendant's discriminatory
> practices complained of herein.

APPENDIX F

74

December 13, 1988 Opinion at 3. The plaintiff class also
includes all members of the 4(a) Subclass certified by the Court
on June 8, 1984 as:

> All past, present and future black employees
> at the Library of Congress ...

> * * *

> who were not promoted to positions by reason
> of the Library of Congress Regulations,
> section 4(a).

June 8, 1984 Opinion at 3-4. If you fall within either, or both,
of the descriptions quoted above and you were employed by the
Library of Congress on or after November 25, 1975, this proposed
settlement may affect you. A Plaintiffs' Committee of up to 13
class members has decided all issues of class membership and
allocation or distribution of the relief provided in the
Agreement. If your name appears on the list of Class Members
compiled by the Plaintiffs' Committee, you have already been
determined to be a member of the class described above.

In lieu of litigation, the parties have arrived at a
proposed settlement in this case that representatives of the
plaintiff class, counsel for the plaintiff class and the
defendant believe is a fair resolution of the class claims.

The Settlement Agreement outlines the procedures the Library
of Congress will follow in its competitive processes for posting
and filling vacancies in professional and administrative
positions. It also provides promotional opportunities for some
class members and monetary payments to class members who qualify
for back pay based on a formula established by the plaintiffs.

- 2 -

Monetary payments will be distributed after final court approval, as stated in the Agreement.

The Settlement Agreement does not represent an admission of liability by defendant, but rather a compromise resolution of the case. Nor does it represent a finding that only a certain number of class members was capable or competent to perform work at a higher level at the Library before or during the pendency of this litigation.

If you are a member of the class on whose behalf this lawsuit was brought, you may submit to the Judge any written comments or objections you may have concerning the proposed settlement. If you choose to submit comments or objections, you must file them in writing and include: (1) a heading that reads "Cook v. Billington, Civil Action No. 82-0400 (NHJ/PJA)" like the one which appears at the top of the first page of this document; (2) your name, address, and telephone number; (3) a specific description of your comments or objections; and (4) a separate, signed statement certifying that you sent copies to counsel for plaintiffs and counsel for defendant and the date that you sent them. You must send an original and two copies of your comments or objections to the Court and one copy each to counsel for plaintiffs and counsel for defendant at the following addresses:

1. UNITED STATES DISTRICT COURT:

> Clerk
> United States District Court
> United States District Courthouse
> 3rd and Constitution Ave., N.W.
> Washington, D.C. 20001

- 3 -

2.   COUNSEL FOR PLAINTIFFS:

        MARC L. FLEISCHAKER
        DAVID L. KELLEHER
        MINDY L. KLASKY
        Arent Fox Kintner
            Plotkin & Kahn
        1050 Connecticut Ave., N.W.
        Washington, D.C. 20036

3.   COUNSEL FOR DEFENDANT:

        MADELYN E. JOHNSON
        Assistant United States Attorney
        555 Fourth Street, N.W.
        Tenth Floor
        Washington, D.C. 20001

Your comments or objections must be received by

_____, 1994 in order to be considered by the Court.

If you live within 50 miles of the District Court, you must also

appear in person to present your comments or objections orally at

a hearing which will be held to consider whether the proposed

settlement should be made final. That hearing will be held

before Judge Norma H. Johnson at _____ on _____, in

Courtroom No. ___ at the United States Courthouse at the above

address. If you wish, you may retain, at your own expense, your

own attorney to represent you in making written comments and/or

objections or at the hearing.

After the hearing, Judge Johnson will decide whether to give

the Settlement Agreement final approval. If you think you are a

class member but your name is not on the attached class list, or

if your name is on the list but you do not think you are a class

member, you must notify plaintiffs' counsel (whose names and

address appear above) by _____. Any challenges

- 4 -

regarding class membership must be filed with the Court by _____

_____, the same date as for filing objections to the

Agreement and you must follow the same procedure. Copies must

also be sent to plaintiffs' counsel and to the Library's counsel

at the addresses listed above.

This is only a brief summary of the terms of the Settlement

Agreement. You should carefully read the Agreement to learn all

of the details of the Agreement.

Enclosed are: (1) a copy of the proposed Settlement

Agreement, (2) copies of all attachments to the Agreement, and

(3) a copy of the final report of the Plaintiffs' Committee.

For further information concerning the proposed settlement

you should contact, as soon as possible, any of the following

attorneys:

MARC L. FLEISCHAKER
DAVID L. KELLEHER
MINDY L. KLASKY
Arent Fox Kintner
    Plotkin & Kahn
1050 Connecticut Ave., N.W.
Washington, D.C. 20036
(202) 857-6000

JOSEPH M. SELLERS
AVIS E. BUCHANAN
Washington Lawyers
  Committee for Civil
  Rights and
  Urban Affairs
1300 Nineteenth Street, N.W.
Suite 500
Washington, D.C. 20036
(202) 835-0031

*   *   *

- 5 -

The Court hereby grants preliminary approval to the Settlement. A Fairness Hearing shall be conducted at _____ o'clock on _____, 1994 in Courtroom No. ____, United States Courthouse, 3rd and Constitution Avenue, N.W., Washington, D.C. 20001. Objections to the Settlement must be filed in writing, in the manner described in this Notice, by _____-_____.

_____
Norma Holloway Johnson
United States District Judge

DATED: This _____ day of _____, 1994.

- 6 -

DISTRIBUTION OF ATTORNEYS' FEES

Law Firm	Settlement Amount of Fees
Arent Fox	$1,092,503.10
Dow Lohnes	$14,000.00
Hogan & Hartson	$24,066.45
Katz	$30,000.00
Mayer Brown	$56,000.00
Mosher	$20,000.00
Perkins Coie	$3,000.00
Sachs Greenbaum & Taylor	$26,000.00
Steptoe	$64,550.12
Washington Lawyers Committee	$190,000.00
Wilmer Cutler	$126,000.00

APPENDIX G

Arent Fox
1050 Connecticut Avenue, NW
Washington, DC 20036-5339

Marc L. Fleischaker
Tel: 202/857-6053
Fax: 202/857-6395

July 27, 1994

John D. Bates, Esq.
Chief, Civil Division
U.S. Department of Justice
U.S. Attorney, District of Columbia
555 4th Street, N.W.
Washington, DC 20001

Re: <u>Cook, et al.</u> v. <u>Billington</u>, United States District Court
for the District of Columbia, Civil Action No. 82-0400

Dear Mr. Bates:

You have requested that we set forth our position in writing relative to the issue of
opt-outs in the settlement of this class action. We have agreed that (1) the settlement
agreement will be silent on the issue of opt-outs; (2) we will not advocate opt-outs to
class members; (3) we will state to the Court the settlement is fair and reasonable to
the class as a whole and that we do not represent individual class members; and that
we cannot advise on the fairness or legality of opting out for any individual class
member; (4) we will advise class members who may wish to opt-out that they may
make that request to the Court, but that we will not represent them; and (5) if asked by
the Court on the law surrounding the issue of opt-outs we will state that the Court may
have the discretion to allow opt-outs in certain circumstances (see, e.g., <u>County of
Suffolk v. Long Island Lighting Co.</u>, 907 F.2d 1295 (2d Cir. 1990)), but counsel is not
aware of any ruling in this Circuit specifically addressing this issue.

Sincerely,

Marc L. Fleischaker

APPENDIX H

Arent Fox Kintner Plotkin & Kahn • Washington, DC
New York, NY • Vienna, VA • Bethesda, MD • Budapest, Hungary • Jeddah, Kingdom of Saudi Arabia

81

CHAPTER
4

SEVEN OTHER EMPLOYEE ORGANIZATIONS IN THE LIBRARY OF CONGRESS

There were seven other employee organizations in the Library of Congress—three (3) unions and four (4) cultural and professional. The three labor unions were Local 2477 American Federation of State, County, and Municipal Employees (AFSCME), Local 2910 AFSCME, and the Congressional Research Service Employee Association (CREA). Cultural and professional organizations included Blacks in Government (BIG), the Daniel A. P. Murray Association (black employees), the Library of Congress Professional Association (LCPA), and the Welfare Recreation Association (WRA). Neither the labor unions nor the cultural and professional organizations helped with the class action over the entire life of the case at the Library of Congress or in the U.S. District Court for the District of Columbia. The class action spanned over a period of time of more than twenty (20) years. At least one of the Locals of AFSCME attempted to intervene after the court rendered its decisions in favor of the plaintiffs. However, we, the plaintiffs opposed the Union's motion to intervene. The court agreed with the plaintiffs after asking the Union where it had been for the last 5, 10, or 15 years.

In 1975 or early 1976, the LOC management along with the labor unions started a program of exclusivity. This was another form of labor segregation. All of the labor unions supported exclusivity, and the other organizations did not say or do anything against the new form of segregation.

The LOC management used the new form of segregation to keep the Black Employees of the Library of Congress (BELC) from holding meetings in the LOC or from using anything else in the LOC. The BELC could not even meet in the cafeteria during lunchtime or breaks. The other organizations, all of them, didn't even say a word. All seven other employee organizations in the LOC failed ethical, legal, moral, and professional tests in their refusal to support the Black Employees of the Library of Congress.

CHAPTER
5

OFFICE CONSPIRACIES

The Equal Employment Opportunity Commission (EEOC) office held the case for seven (7) years claiming to be investigating the facts of the case, always keeping their work top-secret from Howard Cook and David Andrews (plaintiffs). The EEOC never issued a decision in the case to the best knowledge of the author of this book. Even if they did, it did not favor the Black Employees of the Library of Congress. The EEOC has always been there to support the management rather than assure equal opportunity for the employees. That is still its purpose.

There is one other department and three other offices in the LOC that do serious harm to African American employees and minority employees seeking equal employment opportunities in the LOC—the Human Resources department (HR), Office of the Librarians, Office of General Counsel (OGC), and the Health Services (HS) office.

The Department of Human Resources was always up to invalid and illegal posting requirements for jobs—publicizing the positions but making them specifically available for selected employees. This practice was done jointly with the hiring division or department. This was one of the complaints noted in the <u>Howard R.L. Cook, et al. v. Daniel J. Boorstin/James H. Billington</u>, 82-0400 civil case, which the employees won. The only intent of the offices in the LOC was to wind down the clock on the employees.

The system did not work as it is today and never has. Discrimination continues at full speed despite it being illegal. This author does not know of anyone ever being punished for this illegal conduct. (See Chapter 9, Law Upside-Down).

The Librarians' Office never attempts to resolve a problem between the parties. When the black, involved employees contact the office, the Librarian forwards the employees' concerns to the Office of General Counsel (OGC), which is the office that has caused the employee to contact the Librarian in the first place. When these employees contact the OGC, the issue is returned to the EEOC office, which caused the problem in the first place. Thus, the EEOC refers the employees' concerns back to the OGC. The three offices decide to do nothing. The employee is forced to face a hearing examiner or the U.S. District Court for the District of Columbia, which takes forever; and the employee is left with no protection. It is impossible to get the U.S. District Court to provide protection for the employees; thus, rendering Title VII of the Civil Rights Act of 1964 and its amendments meaningless and allows the employer to destroy the employee.

The Health Services office is an arm of the LOC or management. The HS practices illegal medicine. For example, it works to undermine the employees' private doctors' opinions even though the HS never examined or treated these employees. The HS office is not required to provide either service. They would, however, refer the employees to doctors that the LOC has chosen. This puts the employees in a web (figuratively speaking). The author refers to this practice as "illegal medicine."

The Labor Relations office spends all its time attempting to prevent the union contracts from being enforced. The author was contacted by a current employee of the LOC. Based on our conversation, I advised the individual to contact the Labor Relations Office. The employee responded, "I cannot get no help from them." There isn't any office in the LOC from which an employee can get meaningful help. These offices work in a great conspiracy against the employee.

The Equal Employment office in the Library of Congress, the Office of General Counsel, the Office of the Librarian of Congress, and the Department of Justice lost the Cook case to the plaintiffs and continues to lose cases because the discrimination is so deep in the LOC, which is widespread.

It is not hard to determine who these office heads are. They have a responsibility under the law. To reach a more perfect union, we must build on what we have, and the Library of Congress is not excluded.

CHAPTER
6

THE BLACK EMPLOYEES OF THE LIBRARY OF CONGRESS (BELC)

The Black Employees of the Library of Congress (BELC) was a recognized employee organization at the LOC for a short time. This was because the BELC met the requirements under the LOC regulations. As a result, the BELC was entitled to dues check-off. The dues set by the BELC was one dollar ($1.00) per week for each member. As many as four hundred (400) employees joined the BELC. There was a sister organization known as the Ethnic Employees of the Library of Congress. This organization shared leadership with the BELC. The EELC was never granted recognition by the LOC because management learned early that they had some interests that were different than the BELC. The LOC management did not want their issues known.

The LOC management set out to destroy the EELC, and did. The president of the EELC was George E. Perry. Perry was destroyed by LOC's management. Howard Cook, George Perry, and Tommy Shaw have done more for the black employees and all other employees of the LOC than anyone else.

The author of this book was an employee of the LOC under Dr. L. Quincy Mumford, Dr. Daniel J. Boorstin, and Dr. James H. Billington, and two acting Librarians of Congress, Mr. John G. Lorenz and Mr. William J. Welsh. None of these librarians did anything to assure real equal employment for African Americans or other minority employees. The present Librarian of Congress, Dr. Carla Hayden has done nothing. Discrimination is as real as ever under her leadership. Employees cannot get any resolutions to their cases. Nothing is done short of the U.S. District Court.

CHAPTER
7

LABOR UNION EXCLUSIVITY

In 1975/1976, the Library of Congress management and the labor unions started to talk about labor management. This meant labor union exclusivity to segregate out the black employees of the LOC BELC. The BELC was forced into an election in one case to seek department-wide election or in all other departments of the LOC to seek election Library-wide. The BELC was a minority employee organization, greatly outnumbered. The LOC hired a labor union umpire, who at a mass meeting of management officials and employees, declared himself not to be biased. However, with all of that, he ruled against the BELC one hundred percent (100%) of the time each motion the BELC made to have smaller units where black employees were in the majority. There was no law that required him to make 100% of his rulings against the BELC. The BELC discovered that the umpire was making decisions against them when he was not at the LOC and that someone else was signing those decisions other than the umpire himself.

The election was held in 1976, and the BELC lost. The LOC, the unions, and all the other employee organizations took this to mean that the BELC should be segregated out of the LOC – and did just that. Despite all of this, the BELC kept on fighting and went on to win the class action lawsuit against the LOC. No other employee organization has been able to do anything to compare with what the BELC did. As of today, the BELC is still an illegal employee organization at the LOC as well as its sister organization, Ethnic Employees of the Library of Congress (EELC).

CHAPTER
8

No Validated Selection Standards

Discrimination within the Library of Congress continues, as it refuses to keep or maintain legal validated selection standards. After the Cook case, the LOC had validated job selection standards for a brief period. This lasted only until the court's oversight period ended. See letter from Christine Mills, et al., dated June 14, 2018, and response from Rachel A. Bouman, Director of Human Resources, LOC on June 19, 2018. The Bouman letter is really an admission that the LOC has no legally validated selection standards. Each LOC labor union received a copy of the Mills letter. No union responded to the Mills letter since it was provided to them. The lack of response from either labor union is evidence they are not unions at all, and they are also arms of management.

OPM'S UNIFORM GUIDELINES AND VALIDATION:
Dr. Shaw's Signal Institutional Contribution

Arguably, the single most important accomplishment of the Cook Class Action litigation was winning from the Library of Congress (LOC) an agreement that the Library would validate its competitive employee testing and selection procedures for professional and administrative positions in accordance with the Office of Personnel Management's (OPM) Uniform Guidelines on Employee Selection Procedures (The Guidelines). The Guidelines apply to only executive branch agencies. Thus, it was a major coup to extract from LOC, a legislative branch agency, an agreement to comply with The Guidelines. It was Dr. Shaw's technical knowledge of industrial psychology, as well as his dogged persistence to pursue this concession from LOC, that largely made this happen.

All employers, including federal sector agencies, may develop nondiscriminatory employee selection rules and procedures, including minimum job requirements and pre-employment tests. The U.S. Supreme Court ruled in 1971 that employer practices in this area that have an adverse impact on protected minorities and which could not be justified by business necessity constituted illegal discrimination under Title VII of the 1964 Civil Rights Act. Congress essentially wrote that Court interpretation into 1972 statutory amendments to Title VII. These legal principles proved so difficult to elaborate and administer that vast differences between the Equal Employment Opportunity Commission (EEOC) and other federal agencies produced two very different sets of guidelines for federal agencies.

The Guidelines are an attempt to create a uniform federal government position in the area of employment practices on grounds of race, color, religion, sex, or national origin. They are highly technical and complex and are based on legal principles consistently upheld by courts and Congress.

The Guidelines do not contain a legal definition of adverse impact; they adopt the so-called "4/5ths" or "80 percent" rule which focuses on discrepancies in an employer's hiring, promotion, and other employment decisions. Under this approach, an employer compares its hiring and promotion rates for different race, gender, and ethnic groups. But the rule is not a strict mathematical formula: falling below the standard is not necessarily a legal violation, while hiring minorities just to meet the "4/5ths rule" does not necessarily allow an employer to evade legal prosecution. An employer's overall track record is considered, including any affirmative action plan and results achieved under that plan. Essentially, a selection procedure that has no adverse impact generally does not violate Title VII, but if adverse impact exists then it must be justified on grounds of business necessity.

If an employer determines that adverse impact exists, it may evade The Guidelines by modifying or eliminating the guilty procedure. Failing modification or elimination, the employer must demonstrate business necessity, which means, typically, that the employer must show a clear relation between performance on the selection procedure (including any test instrument) and performance on the job. This is called "validating" the selection procedure. Validation may be accomplished either by showing a statistical relationship between job performance and scores on a test or other selection procedure, or by showing that a test or selection procedure representatively samples significant parts of the job, or by devising a test or selection procedure to measure the presence and degree of an identified psychological trait which is essential to successful job performance. In conducting a validation study, the employer must consider available alternatives which will achieve any legitimate business purpose with lesser adverse impact. Thus, the employer cannot concentrate solely on establishing the validity of the instrument or procedure which it has been using in the past.

The Guidelines are not an affirmative action law; illegal employer testing and selection procedures cannot masquerade as affirmative action. Testing and selection procedures undertaken to benefit protected minorities and women still may be illegal if there are adverse impacts on, for example, whites in general or white males in particular.

Generally, The Guidelines have been enthusiastically received by industrial psychologists who are experts on testing and validation. Private and state government employers have modeled their rules after The Guidelines. The EEOC, Civil Service Commission, and the Departments of Labor and Justice have adopted The Guidelines. To date, the Library of Congress has refused to honor its contract with the Cook Class and federal district court to validate its test and selection procedures. The Guidelines make cheating, pre-selection, and discrimination more difficult, though not impossible. One can only conclude that LOC is not committed to the rule of law or equal employment opportunity.

June 14, 2018

To: Mr. Edward Jablonski,
            Chief Human Resource Service

From: Christine Mills et al

Subject: **Requirements, Qualifications and Experience Contained in Announcement No: VAR000423, Librarian (Collection Development)**

This memorandum is to challenge the requirements contained in posted announcement VAR000423. The qualifications listed in the requirements for the position do not meet the standards required for legal and valid job selection. The requirements are so general and non-specific so as to leave selection for the position open to discrimination based on race, and other forms of discrimination, without standards for making the selection not based on any measurable standard which would leave the selection open to subjected biases in favor of the selectee.

The education requirements do not indicate how the Library Science education is relevant to the performance of the actual duties of the position. It does not indicate how the Library Science education or possession of equivalent experience and education are related to the performance of the duties of the position. There is no indication that the education requirements are legal or have met any validated job requirements and standard. The completion of one full academic year of graduate study in Library Science in an accredited College or University, in addition to completion of all work required for a bachelor's degree provides no legal or valid standard for such a requirement. It appears that the intention is to go back to the old requirement of one year of time-in-grade requirement. This requirement has been done away with, because the use of it was proven to be discriminatory.

The requirements advertised in Announcement number VAR000423, go far beyond any relevant requirements for the Librarian (Collection Development) GS-9 position. The requirements are illegal and invalid standards to fill a GS-9 level position.

The position Announcement number VAR000423, contains too many qualifications and requirements each one different to the other. This deems the qualifications and requirements not to be legal, and not have been validated according to any objective standards. No applicant could know if he or she were qualified for the position according to the qualifications and requirements. The substitutes are so broad that the selection process is wide open to discrimination and subjective selection because no legal or valid standards have been applied pertaining to the performance of duties for the position. The qualifications call for education in Library Science or possession of equivalent experience or education, completion of one full year of graduate study in Library Science in an accredited college or university, completion of all work required for a bachelor's degree, a total combination of at least five(5) years of a college level education, training, and experience, knowledge and understanding of theories, principles, and techniques of professional librarianship, knowledge of literature resources, knowledge

95

and abilities essential for providing effective library and information services. There are no, objective measurements for these requirements listed in the announcement. There is no way to have directly related education and or specialized experience unless you have worked in the Library of Congress, two(2) full years progressively higher level graduate education or master's in Library Science or equivalent graduate degree, such as L.L.B, or J.D. related to the position. The announcement makes the claim that the L.L.B. or J.D degree is related the position. Once again there is no, legal or valid criteria to make this claim. There appears to be no standard or valid process to measure maintenance in relationship and consultation liaison services ability to communicate effectively in writing or the ability to communicate effectively other than in writing. None of the other qualifications called for appear to have the abilities to be subjected to any legal or validated standard.

The qualifications and requirements listed in announcement number 000423 do not conform with, **Howard R.L. Cook et al v Daniel Boorstin/James H. Billington 82-0400 D.D.C.** Court Case. **See** the Settlement Agreement in **Cook v Billington.** Nor, do they conform with; **McDonald Douglas 411 US, (1973); Texas Department of Community Affairs v Burdine US, (1981); U.S Postal Service Board of Governors v Aikens, (1983); Furnco Construction Co. v Waters US (1978); Griggs v Duke Power Co. (1971), US.** Title VII of the Civil Rights Act of 1964, as amended by the **Civil Act of 1991.** Nor, do the qualifications and requirements contained in the announcement conform with; **LCR 2010-3.1 and LCR 2010-2.** Most importantly the qualifications and requirements do not conform, with the Supreme Court Decisions on the matter.

No office established in the Library of Congress pertaining to helping employees does so. This is true because all of the offices are creatures of management. These offices are the Equal Employment Office, Office of General Counsel, Labor Relations Office, Health Services Office and Dispute Resolution Office. All these offices are within the Library of Congress. The Equal Employment Office works overtime to obstruct the processing of employees discrimination complaints. The Office of General Counsel does all it can to aid the Equal Employment Opportunity Office in obstructing the processing of the Equal Employment Office complaints. Labor Relation Office joins whatever management wants them to do, the Health Services Office, practices illegal medicine by ruling against what the private doctors of the employees recommend and supports management in its efforts to work against the employees in spite of the private doctors' recommendations, and the Dispute Resolution Office is all but meaningless. When all is said and done the employees lose. African American employees suffer the greatest impact from this system. African American employees are subjected to more harsh adverse actions than other employees.

The Black Employees of the Library of Congress (B.E.L.C.) is the only employee Organization at the Library of Congress, which has never been recognized by the Administration as an Employee Organization. The Black Employee of the Library of Congress (B.E.L.C.) brought the Cook Class Action against the Library of Congress and won. The Class Action Case was **Howard R.L. Cook at el v James H. Billington, Librarian of Congress, 82-0400.** No other employee organization at the Library of Congress joined the Class Action. As, a result of the Class Action the Howard R.L. Cook and Tommy Shaw Foundation at the Library of Congress was formed by the U.S. District Court for District of Columbia.

2

96

The Foundation is recognized, by the Combined Federal Campaign (C.F.C.) and the Internal Revenue Service as well as the Merit System Protection Board. Because, of this the Foundation is permitted to engaged in fund-raising one day per year at the Combine Federal Campaign (C.F.C.) fair. The Foundation is treated differently than the Library of Congress Professional Association, which appears to have free run to engage in fund-raising. The Black Employees of the Library of Congress was established in 1970, and held its first demonstration in 1971, against racial discrimination at the Library of Congress.

We hope the contents of this memorandum will be taken in the right spirit of the Law, and that corrective action will be taken.

Ex. 1 Announcement Number VAR000423
Ex. 2 Position Description for Job Listed

Sincerely,

Christine Mills

Christine Mills, et al

3

Howard R.L. Cook

William Rowland

Carolyn Fosell

Clark Brown

[signature]

[signature]

cc: Dr. Carla Hayden, Librarian of Congress
       Hon. Cedric L. Richmond, (D-LA) Chairman of Congressional Black Caucus
       Hon. Gregg Harper, (R-MS) Chairman of Joint Committee of the Library
       Hon. Robert Brady, (D-PA)   Chairman of Committee of the Library
       Sen. Benjamin Cardin (D-MD)
       Denise Clark, Esq.
       Marc L Fleischaker, Esq.
       Katherine L. Garrett, Esq.
       Daryl Clark, President of AFSCME Local 2477
       Saul Schniderman , President of AFSCME 2910
       Susan Thaul, President of CREA

4

Librarian (Collection Development)

LEGISLATIVE BRANCH
Library of Congress

Overview

Open & closing dates
04/04/2018 to 04/25/2018

Salary
$56,233 to $73,105 per year

Pay scale & grade
GS 09

Work schedule
Full-Time - Flexitime.

Appointment type
Permanent

Locations

1 vacancy in the following location:

Washington DC, DC
1 vacancy

Relocation expenses reimbursed
No

This job is open to

 The public
U.S. citizens, nationals or those who owe allegiance to the U.S.

Announcement number
VAR000423

Control number
495899600

Ex. 1

Duties

Summary

THIS VACANCY REPLACES VACANCY ANNOUNCEMENT NUMBER VAR000382. Those candidates who have applied under Vacancy Announcement Number VAR000382 will not be considered and must reapply.

This position is located in the Collection Development Office, Library Services, and reports to the Collection Development Officer. The incumbent in this position contributes to the Library of Congress's mission to acquire, manage, preserve, and make available a universal collection of knowledge to meet the current and anticipated needs of Congress and the Nation. The incumbent works with guidance from senior analysts in the Collection Development Office (CDO) to conduct in-depth studies, recommend strategies to strengthen acquisition efforts in specific subjects and/or formats, and communicate trends to managers and staff in relevant offices throughout the Library and other external organizations.

This position is located in the Collection Development Office, Library Services.

The position description number for this position is 313241.

The salary range indicated reflects the locality pay adjustments for the Washington, D.C., Metropolitan area.

This is a non-supervisory, bargaining unit position.

Relocation expenses will not be authorized for the person(s) selected under this vacancy announcement.

Responsibilities

The incumbent participates in systematic studies to determine the strengths and weaknesses of collections focusing on a specific subject or format, identifying trends and recommending strategies to enhance the Library's collections in an assigned subject and/or format.

Following approved collections analysis protocol, collaborates with others to prepare and conduct collection development studies that include emerging trends in information dissemination factoring in the needs of users, including Congress, and the anticipated needs of future users.

Identifies scope and depth of assigned collections based on collecting levels articulated in collection development policy statements, collections usage, comparisons with other national and leading academic and research libraries/information centers, available lists, and catalogs and bibliographies of available information resources.

Utilizes internal and external collections databases such as integrated library systems, OCLC, and World Cat to participate in systematic studies to determine the strengths and weaknesses of collections focusing on a specific subject matter or format. Identifies trends and recommends strategies to enhance the Library's collections.

Updates a variety of documents related to collection development and acquisitions for internal and external audiences of varying interests using word processing, spreadsheets, and public presentation software such as PowerPoint.

Represents the Collection Development Office in meetings, conferences, and programs. Serves on cross-organizational committees, task forces, and other focus groups of staff and/or managers convened to address general collection development issues. Promotes Library of Congress collection development policies and practices to internal stakeholders at appropriate fora.

Identifies and reports issues impacting effective and efficient collection development to senior collections development analysts.

Travel Required

Not required

Supervisory status	**Promotion Potential**
No	13

Who May Apply

This job is open to...

Anyone may apply - By law, employment at most U.S. Government agencies, including the Library of Congress, is limited to U.S. citizens. However, non-citizens may be hired, provided that other legal requirements are met and the Library determines there are no qualified U.S. citizens available for the position.

Questions? This job is open to 1 group.

Job family (Series)

1410 Librarian
(https://www.usajobs.gov//Search/?j=1410)

Requirements

Conditions Of Employment

No additional requirements to those listed above.

Qualifications

Applicants must have had progressively responsible experience and training sufficient in scope and quality to furnish them with an acceptable level of the following knowledge, skills, and abilities to perform the duties of the position without more than normal supervision.

Knowledge of the principles and techniques of collection development.**

Ability to use integrated library systems, library applications, or other information technologies.

Ability to analyze and organize information and materials, as well as interpret data, related to collection development.

Ability to develop and maintain relationships and provide consultation and liaison services.**

Ability to communicate effectively in writing.**

Ability to communicate effectively other than in writing.

Education

All librarians must meet the requirements for professional education in library science or possess equivalent experience and education.

1. Completion of 1 full academic year of graduate study in library science in an accredited college or university, in addition to completion of all work required for a bachelor's degree;

or

1. A total of at least 5 years of a combination of college-level education, training, and experience. To qualify on this basis, the applicant must establish conclusively that the education, training, and experience provided knowledge and understanding of the theories, principles, and techniques of professional librarianship; a knowledge of literature resources; and the knowledge and abilities essential for providing effective library and information services.

In addition to meeting the basic entry qualification requirements, applicants must have directly related education and/or specialized experience.

Two full years of progressively higher level graduate education or master's in library science or equivalent graduate degree, e.g., LL.B. or J.D., related to the position.

Additional information

Although it is the Library's policy to afford the maximum pay benefit to employees when setting rates of pay, a new appointee who has had no previous Federal service will generally be paid the minimum step of the grade.

The Library of Congress is an equal opportunity employer. Women, minorities, and persons with disabilities who meet eligibility requirements are strongly encouraged to apply.

Applicants must submit a complete application package that is received by the closing date of this announcement.

This agency provides reasonable accommodation to applicants with disabilities. If you need a reasonable accommodation for any part of the application and hiring process, please ADA@loc.gov. The decision on granting reasonable accommodation will be determined on a case-by-case basis.

Applicants with disabilities may be considered under special hiring procedures and must submit an appropriate certificate of eligibility when applying for this position. The certificate of disability must verify that the applicant has a severe disability and may be issued by a State Vocational Rehabilitation Office, a Disability Services or Career Services Office of the applicant's college or university, or the Department of Veterans Affairs. The date of certification must be within three (3) years of the vacancy closing date and must be submitted with your application. For more information contact the Library's Office of Equal Employment Opportunity and Diversity Programs at 202-707-3960 or email spp@loc.gov. FAILURE TO SUBMIT YOUR CERTIFICATION WILL CAUSE YOUR APPLICATION TO NOT BE CONSIDERED UNDER THE SELECTIVE PLACEMENT PROGRAM.

The Library of Congress is the national library of the United States and is part of the Legislative Branch of the Federal government. As such, all positions are in the excepted service.

Appointment/retention is subject to a favorable evaluation of an appropriate personnel security/suitability investigation.

The Library reserves the right to fill a lesser or greater number of vacancies indicated during the life of this vacancy announcement.

Initial appointments, permanent or indefinite, to the Library of Congress require completion of a one-year probationary period.

A "Not to Exceed" (NTE) status is used to identify an appointment with a specific ending date. However, the Library has the right to separate a NTE employee at any time due to either performance issues or budget constraints.

Are you a veteran? Please indicate the type of veterans' preference you are claiming in your application materials and/or applicant profile and provide the appropriate supporting documentation to validate your claim. Those applying for 5-point preference must submit Member Copy 4 of your DD 214. Those applying for 10-point preference must fill out an SF-15 (click here

(http://www.opm.gov/forms/pdf_fill/SF15.pdf)
for the form) and provide the required documentation listed on the back of the form. If required supporting documentation is not attached, Veterans' Preference will not be considered in the application process.

For more information regarding eligibility requirements, please see the Library of Congress Merit Selection Plan, Section X.D, at: http://www.loc.gov/hr/employment/msp010909.pdf (http://www.loc.gov/hr/employment/msp010909.pdf)

How You Will Be Evaluated

The Library of Congress evaluates applicants through an applicant questionnaire and a structured interview. Applicants may also be screened for some jobs through licensing, certification, and/or education requirements, a narrative/application review, and/or a preliminary telephone interview. The knowledge, skills, and abilities (KSAs) that are marked with a double asterisk (**) in the vacancy announcement and the applicant questionnaire are considered the most critical for a position. To be considered for final selection, applicants must demonstrate fully acceptable experience in these designated KSAs in the narrative/application review, preliminary telephone and/or full structured interview. The various assessment tools listed above are designed to verify or explore applicants' experience, knowledge, and training directly related to the job in order to identify the best qualified applicants for selection.
To preview questions please click here
(https://jobs.monstergovt.com/loc/vacancy/previewVacancyQuestions.hms?orgId=1&jnum=24668)

Background checks and security clearance

Security clearance

Not Applicable
(https://www.usajobs.gov/Help/faq/job-announcement/security -clearances/)

Required Documents

Current or former federal employees must submit their most recent Notification of Personnel Action (SF-50 or equivalent). Disabled applicants claiming Selective Placement eligibility must submit proof of disability and a certification of job readiness. If Selective Placement is applicable to you, you will not be considered without submitting this documentation.

If you are relying on your education to meet qualification requirements:

Education must be accredited by an accrediting institution recognized by the U.S. Department of Education in order for it to be credited towards qualifications. Therefore, provide only the attendance and/or degrees from schools accredited by accrediting institutions recognized by the U.S. Department of Education (http://www.ed.gov/admins/finaid/accred/)

Failure to provide all of the required information as stated in this vacancy announcement may result in an ineligible rating or may affect the overall rating.

Benefits

A career with the U.S. Government provides employees with a comprehensive benefits package. As a federal employee, you and your family will have access to a range of benefits that are designed to make your federal career very rewarding.

- Benefits for federal employees

(https://www.usa.gov/benefits-for-federal-employees#item-36407)

- Healthcare insurance
  (https://www.opm.gov/healthcare-insurance/)

○ Pay and leave
  (https://www.usajobs.gov/Help/working-in-government/pay-and-leave/)

https://www.loc.gov/careers/working-at-the-library/benefits/

Eligibility for benefits depends on the type of position you hold and whether your position is full-time, part-time, or intermittent. Contact the hiring agency for more information on the specific benefits offered.

How to Apply

Please carefully follow all instructions under the How to Apply tab to ensure you are considered for the position. You are required to apply online for this announcement. We are unable to accept mailed or emailed documents. You must complete the entire application process, including submission of all documents BEFORE this announcement closes. To do so, complete the following steps.

Step 1: If you do not already have one, create a resume on USAJOBS. Although you must enter your Social Security Number for USAJOBS, this information will not be provided to the Library of Congress.

Step 2: Review the Job Announcement. We recommend you go to the end of the Qualification and Evaluation section of the job announcement to preview the online questions that you will answer in Step 4. You may wish to customize your USAJOBS resume to ensure that it supports your responses to these questions.

Step 3: Click on the "APPLY ONLINE" button to the right of this announcement. Follow USAJOBS' instructions to access your account and submit your resume. You will be redirected to the Hiring Management website to complete the application process. If this is your first time in Hiring Management, you will be asked to answer questions related to your eligibility for Federal employment. You will be able to update this information and save it to our account for future announcements.

Step 4: Once you have completed the eligibility questions, you will be taken directly to the vacancy application questions. Answer all questions honestly and thoroughly. Step 5: Hiring Management offers three options that will electronically attach your documentation to your online application once you finish answering the questions in the job announcement.

(1) You may select a document that you have already uploaded to USAJOBS for a previous announcement.

(2) You may electronically upload a document directly from your computer to your application. Be certain to review your complete application for confirmation of the document uploaded and click on "Finished" to be returned to USAJOBS.

(3) You may follow the "Faxing Supporting Documentation" instructions within the online application, which will provide the necessary cover sheets for each of your documents so that they will be correctly submitted. The fax number will be available on the cover sheet.

Please note that each cover sheet and corresponding document must be faxed separately. Be certain to review your complete fax transmittal confirmation to ensure that all pages have been received.

IMPORTANT NOTE: If you have multiple documents of the same kind, e.g. 2 undergraduate transcripts from different schools or 2 SF-50s, etc., be sure that they are all in the same file on your computer or in your USAJOBS profile before uploading them. If you try uploading them individually, only the last one sent will be visible in our system. Likewise, if sending them by fax, be sure and include both of them behind the respective fax cover sheet and send them as one fax. If you send them individually with the same cover sheet, the last one sent will overwrite the first one. Finally, if you upload a document, e.g. your undergraduate transcript, do not also fax that same document (or fax another undergraduate transcript), because whichever one you send last will be the only one that is visible in our system. If you have any questions about this information, please contact the person on this announcement BEFORE the closing date.

Step 6: Click on "Finish" after you have completed your application. Once you have submitted your application, you can check your status online through your Hiring Management or MY USAJOBS account. Your complete online application and any required supplemental documentation (e.g., SF-50, etc.) must be received by 11:59 p.m. Eastern Standard Time (EST) on the closing date of the announcement. It is your responsibility to ensure that all documents are received on time and that the materials are readable. Failure to do so will result in your application being excluded from consideration for this announcement.

If you are experiencing any technical difficulty with the online process, you MUST CONTACT THE POINT OF CONTACT FOR THIS ANNOUNCEMENT BEFORE THE CLOSING DATE. For all technical issues please contact jobhelp@loc.gov , no later than 4:30pm EST of the Closing Date. REQUESTS FOR EXTENSIONS WILL NOT BE GRANTED.

Agency contact information

👤 Customer Service Center

Phone

202-707-5620
(tel://202-707-5620)

Fax

000-000-0000

Email

JobHelp@loc.gov
(mailto:JobHelp@loc.gov)

Learn more about this agency
(#agency-modal-trigger)

Address

LIBRARY OF CONGRESS
101 Independence Ave. SE
LM-107
Washington, District of Columbia
United States

Visit our careers page

Learn more about what it's like to work at Library of Congress, what the agency does, and about the types of careers this agency offers.

https://jobs.monstergovt.com/loc/vacancy/preview.hms?orgId=1&jnum=24668#overview/
(https://jobs.monstergovt.com/loc/vacancy/preview.hms?orgId=1&jnum=24668#overview)

Next steps

Please review our evaluation process under Evaluation. You may check the status of your application for this position at any time by logging onto the USAJOBS "My USAJOBS" tab and clicking on "My Applications." You will receive final notification via e-mail when the vacancy has been filled.

Fair & Transparent

The Federal hiring process is setup to be fair and transparent. Please read the following guidance.

Equal Employment Opportunity Policy

The United States Government does not discriminate in employment on the basis of race, color, religion, sex (including pregnancy And gender identity), national origin, political affiliation, sexual orientation, marital status, disability, genetic information, age, membership in an employee organization, retaliation, parental status, military service, or other non-merit factor.

- Equal Employment Opportunity (EEO) office at OPM
  (https://www.opm.gov/about-us/our-people-organization/support-functions/equal-employment-opportunity/)
- Office of Equal Opportunity
  (http://www.eeoc.gov/eeoc/internal_eeo/index.cfm)

Reasonable Accommodation Policy

Federal agencies must provide reasonable accommodation to applicants with disabilities where appropriate. Applicants requiring reasonable accommodation for any part of the application and hiring process should contact the hiring agency directly. Determinations on requests for reasonable accommodation will be made on a Case-by-Case basis.

A reasonable accommodation is any change in the workplace or the way things are customarily done that provides an equal employment opportunity to an individual with a disability. Under the Rehabilitation Act of 1973 the Equal Employment Opportunity Commission (EEOC) must provide reasonable accommodations:

- An applicant with a disability needs an accommodation to have an equal opportunity to apply for a job.
- An employee with a disability needs an accommodation to perform the essential job duties or to gain access to the workplace.
- An employee with a disability needs an accommodation to receive equal access to benefits, such as details, training, and office-sponsored events.
- Disability Employment - Reasonable Accommodations (https://www.opm.gov/policy-data-oversight/disability-employment/reasonable-accommodations/)
- How to contact an agency (https://www.usajobs.gov//Help/how-to/application/agency/contact/)

Legal and regulatory guidance

Financial suitability
(https://www.usajobs.gov//Help/working-in-government/fair-and-transparent/financial-suitability/)

Social security number request
(https://www.usajobs.gov//Help/working-in-government/fair-and-transparent/social-security-number/)

Privacy Act
(https://www.usajobs.gov//Help/working-in-government/fair-and-transparent/privacy-act/)

Signature & False statements
(https://www.usajobs.gov//Help/working-in-government/fair-and-transparent/signature-false-statements/)

Selective Service
(https://www.usajobs.gov//Help/working-in-government/fair-and-transparent/selective-service/)

New employee probationary period
(https://www.usajobs.gov//Help/working-in-government/fair-and-transparent/probationary-period/)

POSITION DESCRIPTION *(Please Read Instructions on the Back)*

	1. Agency Position No.
	313341

2. Reason for Submission	3. Service	4. Employing Office Location	5. Duty Station	6. OPM Certification No.
☑ Redescription ☐ New ☑ Hdqrs ☐ Field		Washington, DC	Washington, DC	

☐ Reestablishment ☐ Other	7. Fair Labor Standards Act	8. Financial Statements Required	9. Subject to IA Action
_xplanation (Show any positions replaced)	☑ Exempt ☐ Nonexempt	☐ Executive Personnel Financial Disclosure ☐ Employment and Financial Interest	☑ Yes ☐ No

	10. Position Status	11. Position is	12. Sensitivity	13. Competitive Level Code
	☐ Competitive	☐ Supervisory	☑ 1–Non-Sensitive ☐ 3–Critical	
	☑ Excepted *(Specify in Remarks)*	☐ Managerial		14. Agency Use
	☐ SES (Gen.) ☐ SES (CR)	☑ Neither	☐ 2–Noncritical Sensitive ☐ 4–Special Sensitive	P

15. Classified/Graded by	Official Title of Position	Pay Plan	Occupational Code	Grade	Initials	Date
a. Office of Personnel Management						
b. Department, Agency or Establishment	Librarian (Collection Development)	GS	1410	09	LOM	5/12/2014
c. Second Level Review						
d. First Level Review						
e. Recommended by Supervisor or Initiating Office						

16. Organizational Title of Position (if different from official title)	17. Name of Employee (if vacant, specify)
Collections Development Analyst	

18. Department, Agency, or Establishment	c. Third Subdivision
Library of Congress	Collection Development Office
a. First Subdivision	d. Fourth Subdivision
Library Services	
b. Second Subdivision	e. Fifth Subdivision
Office of the Associate Librarian	

i. Employee Review-This is an accurate description of the major duties and responsibilities of my position.

Signature of Employee (optional)

20. Supervisory Certification. *I certify that this is an accurate statement of the major duties and responsibilities of this position and its organizational relationships, and that the position is necessary to carry out Government functions for which I am responsible. This certification is made with the knowledge that* this information is to be used for statutory purposes relating to appointment and payment of public funds, and that false or misleading statements may constitute violations of such statutes or their implementing regulations.

a. Typed Name and Title of Immediate Supervisor	b. Typed Name and Title of Higher-Level Supervisor or Manager (optional)
Joseph Puccio	Roberta I. Shaffer
Collection Development Officer	Associate Librarian for Library Services
Signature *Joseph Puccio*	Date 16/10/13	Signature *Robert Shaffer*	Date 7/26/2013

21. Classification/Job Grading Certification. *I certify that this position has been classified/graded as required by Title 5, U.S. Code, in conformance with standards published by the U.S. Office of Personnel Management or, if no published standards apply directly, consistently with the most applicable published standards.*

22. Position Classification Standards Used in Classifying/Grading Position
Librarian Series, 1410, TS-130, Aug 1994

Typed Name and Title of Official Taking Action
Lvashawnne O. Malachi
Position Classification Specialist
Signature *Lvashawnne O. Malachi*	Date 5/12/14

Information for Employees. The standards, and information on their application, are available in the personnel office. The classification of the position may be reviewed and corrected by the agency or the U.S. Office of Personnel Management. Information on classification/job grading appeals, and complaints on exemption from FLSA, is available from the personnel office or the U.S. Office of Personnel Management.

23. Position Review	Initials	Date	Initials	Date	Initials	Date	Initials	Date	Initials	Date
a. Employee (optional)										
b. Supervisor										
c. Classifier										

24. Remarks q/12/13 Position established as part of 2013 reorganization

In promotion plan with: GS-1410-13-313344 , GS-1410-12-313243 , GS-1410-11-313242

Description of Major Duties and Responsibilities (See Attached)

NSN 7540-00-634-4265	Previous Edition Usable	5008-106	OF 8 (Rev. 1-85) U.S. Office of Personnel Management FPM Chapter 295

Ex. 2

LIBRARIAN (COLLECTION DEVELOPMENT)
GS-1410-09

Position Number: 313241

Introductory Statement:

This position is located in the Collection Development Office, Library Services, and reports to the Collection Development Officer. The incumbent in this position contributes to the Library of Congress's mission to acquire, manage, preserve, and make available a universal collection of knowledge to meet the current and anticipated needs of Congress and the Nation. The incumbent works with guidance from senior analysts in the Collection Development Office (CDO) to conduct in-depth studies, recommend strategies to strengthen acquisition efforts in specific subjects and/or formats, and communicate trends to managers and staff in relevant offices throughout the Library and other external organizations.

Collections Development Analysis: 50%

The incumbent participates in systematic studies to determine the strengths and weaknesses of collections focusing on a specific subject or format, identifying trends and recommending strategies to enhance the Library's collections in an assigned subject and/or format. Following approved collections analysis protocol, collaborates with others to prepare and conduct collection development studies that include emerging trends in information dissemination factoring in the needs of users, including Congress, and the anticipated needs of future users. Identifies scope and depth of assigned collections based on collecting levels articulated in collection development policy statements, collections usage, comparisons with other national and leading academic and research libraries/information centers, available lists, and catalogs and bibliographies of available information resources. Utilizes internal and external collections databases such as integrated library systems, OCLC, and World Cat to participate in systematic studies to determine the strengths and weaknesses of collections focusing on a specific subject matter or format. Identifies trends and recommends strategies to enhance the Library's collections. Compiles, manipulates, and maintains information using relational databases such as Microsoft Access. Assists senior collection development analysts, curators, subject specialists, and their managers to review, edit, and update collections policy statements and other documentation to ensure currency and accuracy based on changes to policies, practices and trends. Assists with managing collection policy review schedules. Researches collection policy standards based on input from internal and external stakeholders ensuring alignment with Library of Congress and Library Services strategic plans and priorities. Standards reflect collection policies, practices and trends used by other research libraries and information centers. Analysis may include preservation, management, storage and space issues and recommendations, as well as trends in research methods and scholarly communication related to collections development.

Prepares Written Materials: 25%

Updates a variety of documents related to collection development and acquisitions for internal and external audiences of varying interests using word processing, spreadsheets, and public presentation software such as PowerPoint. Prepares narrative and graphical reports relating to the strengths and weaknesses of the Library's collections and acquisition goals. Drafts descriptive memos, correspondence, reports, and other documents that include narrative text graphs, charts, tables, and other visual representations of collection development analysis for review by the senior collections development analysts. Assists in documenting collection policy activities and schedules. Prepares meeting agendas, notes and action items that facilitate the efficient accomplishment of collection development milestone tasks. Prepares weekly, monthly, quarterly, annual, and other production and activity reports of varying frequency highlighting individual and group accomplishments and trends. Maintains documentation relating to collections development.

Consultation and Liaison Activities: 25%

Represents the Collection Development Office in meetings, conferences, and programs. Serves on cross-organizational committees, task forces, and other focus groups of staff and/or managers convened to address general collection development issues. Promotes Library of Congress collection development policies and practices to internal stakeholders at appropriate fora. Committee and task force members may include Collection Development Office staff and/or acquisition, reference, research, and preservation staff of the Library of Congress. Participates in discussions regarding some aspects of collection development policies in the Library of Congress and other libraries/information centers.

Identifies and reports issues impacting effective and efficient collection development to senior collections development analysts. Delivers presentations to individuals and groups, and participates in discussions that identify emerging issues and/or leads to resolution of matters relating to collection development, management, preservation, and/or storage issues. Develops and maintains professional relationships with collection development partners and collaborators, acquisitions, preservation, and reference librarians to understand issues and trends in collection development. Maintains current awareness of issues, practices, trends, and collaborative efforts in collections development, storage,
and preservation.

Other Important Information:

Performs other duties as assigned.

Factor 1-6   Knowledge Required by the Position   950 points

Knowledge of standard methods, techniques, concepts, and principles of one or more specialty areas of librarianship is required to perform independently assignments in locating, classifying, selecting, controlling, or preserving information. Assignments can be successfully performed without significant deviation from established methods and precedents. Assignments usually involve providing professional library services to meet a clientele's nonspecialized needs, such as general reading, viewing videotaped movies or instructional videos, and/or listening to music, literature or instructional material on audio cassette; or they may consist of limited segments of more complex assignments regarding specialized information needs. Assignments are generally characterized by such features as: services and products (e.g., bibliographies, cataloging records) are nontechnical in nature or of limited technical complexity, and seldom require going beyond easily-accessed sources of information; information is obtained, organized, and maintained using standard reference tools and established techniques and practices, such as an overall classification system (e.g., Library of Congress, Dewey Decimal) and cataloging rules with prescribed local modifications, customary reference interviewing techniques, standard search strategies, commonly used bibliographic information sources and professional journals in the library field, or accepted practices for maintaining the quality of contemporary print materials; and participation in formulating plans for collection development, changes in physical facilities, or improved automation services is limited to developing factual data, such as usage statistics for certain journals or books, frequently asked reference questions, or descriptions of problems with particular software.

| Factor 2-3 | Supervisory Controls | 275 points |

The supervisor defines the librarian's scope of responsibility and the objectives, priorities, and deadlines. The librarian is provided with more detailed assistance in unusual situations that do not have clear precedents. The supervisor or a senior librarian provides guidance on difficult decisions or how to locate source materials that are not readily accessible. Work may be assigned as a designated area of ongoing responsibility. The librarian plans and carries out the successive steps, handles deviations from established procedures, and resolves problems that arise in accordance with instructions, policies, previous training, or accepted library practices. Completed work is usually evaluated for technical soundness, appropriateness to the needs of the library and its clientele, and conformity to policy and requirements. The methods used by the librarian in arriving at the end results are not usually reviewed in detail.

| Factor 3-3 | Guidelines | 275 points |

Guidelines include library and agency information policies, regulations, and operating procedures; cataloging rules and formats; authorities lists; subject heading lists; professional and technical literature; accreditation standards; and in some cases, Federal contracting regulations. The guidelines are not completely applicable to the work or have gaps in specificity. For example, classification system policies require some interpretation to cover new and evolving subject matter areas, or as new sources of materials for reference searches become available. The librarian uses judgment in interpreting and adapting the guidelines for application to specific cases, problems, or situations, in applying standard library practices to new situations and in relating new work situations to precedent ones. In addition, the librarian analyzes the results of adaptations and recommends changes or improvements to the guidelines.

| Factor 4-3 | Complexity | 150 points |

Decisions regarding what needs to be done depend on analysis of each objective and the nature of the information to be provided or categorized. Choosing a course of action often involves selecting from many alternatives, including identifying and recommending minor deviations from established practices. Assignments involve identifying and analyzing relationships among the various aspects of library work, such as the effect of decisions on the accessibility of the information by reference librarians and the clientele, and applying standard methods, techniques, and programs. Examples of assignments include searching standard data bases where the information is relatively stable, such as for bibliographic citations of a general nature; cataloging materials that are generally covered by standard subject heading lists and appropriate authority files; and locating and acquiring print and video information.

Factor 5-3   Scope and Effect   150 points

The purpose of the work is to apply established practices and techniques to investigate and analyze a variety of frequently-encountered library problems, questions, or situations such as in the management of a general library, or a definite area of responsibility in public services, technical services, or systems. The librarian recommends solutions or courses of action. The work affects other library personnel, and the ability of clientele to perform their missions. Furnishing accurate, timely, and responsive information enables clientele to accomplish their missions more effectively and/or to derive satisfaction from the enrichment provided.

Factor 6 (Level 2) Personal and Purpose of Contacts

Factor 7 (Level b)   75 points

Contacts are with employees in the same agency, but outside the immediate organization, (e.g., library users, employees engaged in nonlibrary work) and/or individuals or groups outside the agency, such as librarians in other organizations and clientele outside the agency, in a moderately structured setting. Contacts are to plan or coordinate work efforts, solve operating problems, or to provide advice to managers and clientele on noncontroversial issues and concerns.

Factor 8-1   Physical Demands   5 points

The work is sedentary and includes no special physical demands. It may involve some walking, standing, bending, or carrying light items.

Factor 9-1   Work Environment   5 points

Work involves everyday risks or discomforts typically associated with libraries, offices, meeting and training rooms. Work areas are adequately heated, lighted, and ventilated.

Total Points: 1885

Green, Paulette

From: Bouman, Rachel
Sent: Friday, June 15, 2018 5:58 PM
To: Mills, Christine <chmills@loc.gov>
Subject: Response to your letter of June 14, 2018

Dear Ms. Mills:

As the Director for Human Resources Services, I am responding to your letter of June 14, 2018, regarding Vacancy Announcement # VAR000423.

The U.S. Office of Personnel Management (OPM) has a positive educational requirement for the 1410 (Librarian) occupational series. At the Library of Congress, each hiring panel, through job analysis, has the discretion under the Library's Merit Selection Plan to set the qualification standards they feel are appropriate for the position being recruited. (See Merit Selection Plan at section VIII.B.2.) For the position you have referenced and consistent with the discretion under the Merit Selection Plan, the hiring panel adopted OPM's educational requirement.

Sincerely,
Rachel

Rachel A. Bouman
Director, Human Resources Services
Library of Congress

1

CHAPTER
9

LAW UPSIDE-DOWN

This is true because the U.S. Supreme Court places the burden of proof on the employee who knows that he or she has been discriminated against by the employer or whatever the case may be that results in discrimination. The lower courts followed suit in all cases. This places the employee or person in a lone position to defend his or her rights under the law. No justice becomes real until the offender has had time to destroy the offended employee or persons complaining. The system is always upside-down against the one suffering discrimination. The fact is that because the U.S. Supreme Court (nine (9) judges) messes with the law passed by the U.S. Congress House and Senate, you get an upside-down unjust system. It does not matter who is conservative or liberal; they all hold to the same view of the law on this issue. This is why it took so long to get real justice and equal justice in the United States of America. It was never intended.

In class actions, you have to win first then negotiate a settlement with the offender of the law who discriminated against you in the first place. Therefore, you have to negotiate with criminals who have committed the crime against you as to what his punishment should be. The person responsible for writing this book does not know of anyone at the LOC who has been found to have discriminated to be punished or to pay by any means even after the discrimination has hurt a number of people in so many ways.

This book is intended to call for a system of punishment for those breaking the law by discriminating. Are they breaking the law? Their actions deem Title VII and its amendments meaningless. So then, the question becomes, as a nation, are we serious, or have we ever been? The whole U.S. government defends the lawbreakers who break the law. The U.S. courts play the role by their inaction supporting those who break the law. This happens because the discriminators of every lot know that they get away free after causing much money and time to be spent, as well as hurt of many.

This is especially true when it comes to the Federal Government. The Cook case is a prime example. The illegal discrimination continues. The evidence is presented in one place in this book. The three offices in the LOC which do the most harm to African Americans and other minority employees are the Librarian's office, the Office of "Equal Opportunity," and the Office of General Counsel. This has been discussed in prior parts of this book. There are two cases pending before the U.S. District Court for the District of Columbia which cause the writer of this book most concern because of the time it took to get a resolution. They are <u>Christine Mills, et al. v. James H. Billington/Carla Hayden</u>, 04-2205 and <u>Christine Mills v. Carla Hayden</u>, 17-1257. These two cases which joined on a motion by the LOC prove that the court really works to the advantage of the lawbreakers and against the lone employee due to the time it takes the court to provide equal opportunity and justice. The Library's motion to join the two cases was for the purpose of delay only—and it worked. This is an old, old story. As things are, it will take another four hundred (400) years to reach equal opportunity and justice in the United States. There is none in the US today. The writer can say this after more than fifty (50) years of experience.

CHAPTER
10

WORK SLOWDOWN

A group of thirteen (13) deck attendants staged a "work slowdown," complaining about job discrimination in employment (1970). This slowdown was not BELC approved. The BELC learned about it at the same time as all the other employees and employee organizations did. However, the BELC did support all 13 deck attendants—raising funds for them as well as offering legal service assistance. No other employee organizations of the LOC gave any support to the deck attendants. All the deck attendants were fired. They complained about illegal class-wide actions against them, which was discrimination. The "work slowdown" lasted about a week. It was totally passive. It caused this writer to be more determined to do something about the situation of all minority employees at the LOC. Thus, the start of the Cook Class Action in 1975—there was lots of work to be done.

The BELC was started in 1970. The deck attendants' actions did lead to an upgrade in their jobs over time. A sad part of what happened to the attendants was the thirteen had black employees from the EEO go to court and testify against them, as well as other black employees from LOC management and others who worked in EEO. All segments of police in the Washington, D.C. area were called. This included some military. The young deck attendants were arrested, taken to jail, booked, and then court processes began. There were only 13 of the GS-1 and GS-2. African Americans and others received promotions and jobs for their testimony against the deck attendants. When management sanctioned crime adversely affects employees, then the employees should be permitted to strike against the Federal Government and all other forms of government. The deck attendants had been affected adversely by the Federal Government. This alone would put "teeth" in Title VII, agency by agency. Until then, Title VII means almost nothing. No courts should take more than twenty years to resolve discrimination class action lawsuits such as the Cook case or any other discrimination case while minority employees are being discriminated against. To approve a one-promotion settlement agreement in such a case is discrimination. At the same time, the majority of employees have received several promotions over this same period within those twenty years. Minority employees will never catch up or be made whole.

CHAPTER
11

WHAT AN EMPLOYEE SHOULD KNOW

1. Know your rights under Title VII of the Civil Rights Act of 1964.
2. Know what office to complain to at your place of work.
3. Do not believe anything your EEO tells you. They defend the employer.
4. Meet all your filing deadlines.
5. Get a lawyer.
6. Be aware of your employer's regulations on EEO.
7. Expect the U.S. courts and the local courts to take forever to act.
8. Maintain your faith and believe in yourself.
9. Leave the case at work. Do not take it home.

CHAPTER
12

CHRONOLOGY OF COOK CASE

1975: An administrative complaint was filed in the Library of Congress alleging discrimination on the basis of race, national origin, and sex on behalf of all black females, and Spanish-speaking employees and applicants for employment at the Library of Congress. This administrative complaint formed the basis for the 1982 lawsuit.

1982: A lawsuit was filed in the U.S. District Court, District of Columbia, by Howard Cook and a group of black employees against the Library alleging a pattern of discrimination against black employees and black applicants for employment in all personnel actions since 1975. The lawsuit, titled Cook v. Boorstin, was brought under Title VII of the 1964 Civil Rights Act, as amended.

1984: The court certified a group of black employees as a subclass. This subclass alleged that the Library discriminated by filling positions without competition under Section 4(a) of LC Regulation 2010-14.

1987: James H. Billington became Librarian of Congress and the case was renamed Cook v. Billington.

1988: The court enjoined the Library from using its noncompetitive "Section 4(a)" hiring or promotion authority except for limited periods of time. The court certified a class of black employees and allowed consideration of new claims of discrimination against blacks who qualified for professional and administrative positions dating from 1975: (1) competitive selections in professional and administrative positions; (2) noncompetitive promotions, such as career ladder promotions; and (3) other personnel actions such as training and other job-related opportunities.

1992: The court granted the plaintiffs' motion for partial summary judgment based entirely on statistical data from 1979-88. Based on that statistical data, the court found the Library's three-stage selection process to be so "subjective" as to discriminate against black applicants for administrative and professional positions.

1994: Attorneys for the Library and the plaintiffs reached a tentative settlement agreement that provided for a total of $8.5 million in back pay, 40 promotions, and 10 reassignments. Included in the total monetary relief of $8.5 million was a total payment of $805,264.01 - the amount ordered by the court in 1989 - to the 4(a) subclass members.

1995: A four-day fairness hearing was held and nearly 200 individuals objected to the tentative settlement agreement, endorsed by both plaintiffs and Library lawyers after 21 months of negotiation. Members of the plaintiffs' Settlement Committee also testified to explain how they processed 2,134 claims and allocated $8.5 million in back pay, 40 promotions, and 10 reassignments.

U.S. District Court Judge Norma H. Johnson issued final approval of the settlement agreement. She noted that "the sweeping personnel changes at the Library effected by the settlement of this matter are...the primary benefit produced by the Cook litigation." In her written decision, she noted that she would reserve jurisdiction over the action for a four-year period "for the purpose of implementing and assuring compliance with it and resolving disputes..."

1996: The District Court issued an order allowing implementation of the settlement agreement. The settlement agreement became effective 12/1/1996 and was scheduled to expire 12/1/2000.

1998: Plaintiffs filed a motion to enforce the settlement agreement, arguing that the Library had not produced required statistical reports in a timely fashion, that it had not computed the statistical data in compliance with the settlement agreement, and it had not validated its selection procedures correctly. The Library responded that the issues were moot because the Library had complied in all respects with the settlement agreement.

Plaintiffs subsequently filed a motion requesting the court to appoint a receiver within the personnel department of the Library of Congress to implement and to oversee the Library's timely compliance with its obligations under the Settlement Agreement and Consent Decree until the four-year oversight period expired. The Library responded that the agreement had not been breached, that plaintiffs' suggestion that a receiver be appointed had no basis in law; and that plaintiffs failed to abide by the Local Rules of the Court and the explicit terms of the agreement in bringing their motion.

Following a November hearing, Judge Johnson ordered attorneys for both sides "to sit down and resolve their dispute" over methods of reporting personnel selection statistics and validating LC selection procedures, and to report back.

1999*: A status conference was held and the parties reported that they exchanged information and proposals, both in meetings and in writing, but had not been able to resolve their differences. The Library asked the court to appoint a magistrate judge to help the parties resolve their differences. The plaintiffs argued that the dispute should not be referred to a magistrate unless the Library agrees to "stop the clock" on the time frame for which the court has jurisdiction over the case while negotiations proceed. In March, the court appointed Magistrate Judge Alan Kay to assist the parties to resolve their differences and "tolled" the same frame for which the court has jurisdiction of the case.*

2001*: In January, a joint report was filed by counsel for both parties outlining the proposed resolution of the outstanding motions. The court adopted the parties' proposal finding it to be "fair, reasonable, adequate and in the best interest of the Class." The proposal included a new statistical methodology for measuring the selection process and a new competitive selection process.*

In March, the tolling order was lifted and the new selection process was implemented. The portions of the original settlement agreement that were not the subject of the plaintiffs' motion expired Jan. 18 with the court's order; all other aspects of the settlement agreement are scheduled to expire Dec. 1, 2002.

In December, class counsel filed a motion to withdraw, or alternatively to designate substitute class representative.

***2002**: On Jan. 30, 2002, plaintiffs filed a motion requesting an enlargement of time to reply to their counsels' motion. On Jan. 31, 2002, class counsels' motion to withdraw was granted.*

On March 11, 2002, the Library requested that the court's order be amended to provide that Arent Fox remain class counsel until such time as plaintiffs retain - and the court accepts - substitute counsel. On March 15, 2002, a status conference was held and the court granted the Library's motion. The court gave plaintiffs until April 30, 2002, to retain new counsel in the case and scheduled a status conference for May 30, 2002.

At the status conference on May 30, 2002, the court approved the new class counsel, and the case remains active with the court.

Howard R.L. Cook, et al. v.
Daniel J. Boorstin/James H. Billington, 82-0400

CONCLUSION

To the best of the author's knowledge, corruption, discrimination, illegal conduct, mismanagement, misuse of federal and other funds remain an activity at the Library of Congress. There is only a small number of people who have oversight of the LOC. This writer has none and no ability to investigate. Cases of discrimination are still pending in the U.S. District Court for the District of Columbia.

"And Jesus said unto him, No man, having put his hand to the plough, and looking back, is fit for the kingdom of God."
Luke 9:62, King James Version (KJV)

Special Note: If the late Dr. Tommy Shaw was not made "whole" from the Cook case, his family should be, without delay, along with all the benefits he would have received.

The Howard R.L. Cook and Tommy Shaw Foundation for Black Employees of the Library, Inc.

The purposes of the Howard R.L. Cook and Tommy Shaw Foundation for Black Employees of the Library, Inc. are:

To end and deter the effects of racially discriminatory employment practices against African American employees of the Library of Congress.

Provide education and training programs to African American employees of the Library of Congress in the area of professional development such as interviewing, job application techniques, resume writing, and other employment related and job seeking skills.

Aid African American Library of Congress employees pursuing claims of discrimination.

The Howard R. L. Cook and Tommy Shaw Foundation for Black Employees at the Library, Inc. is a 501(c)(3) organization. The original funding of the Foundation came from left over funds from the class action.

The Fight Was Hard!

Made in the USA
Middletown, DE
29 October 2023

41556058R00080